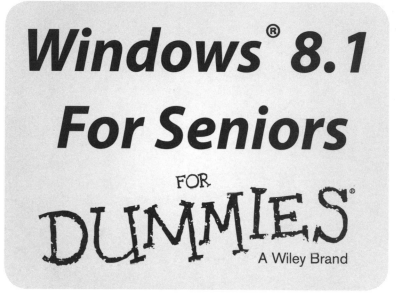

Windows® 8.1
For Seniors

FOR

DUMMIES®

A Wiley Brand

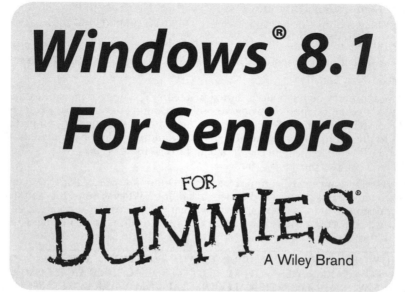

Windows® 8.1 For Seniors

FOR

DUMMIES®

A Wiley Brand

by Peter Weverka and Mark Justice Hinton

Windows® 8.1 For Seniors For Dummies®

Published by: **John Wiley & Sons, Inc.,** 111 River Street, Hoboken, NJ 07030-5774, www.wiley.com

Copyright © 2014 by John Wiley & Sons, Inc., Hoboken, New Jersey

Media and software compilation copyright © 2014 by John Wiley & Sons, Inc. All rights reserved.

Published simultaneously in Canada

Contents at a Glance

Table of Contents

*W*indows 8.1 is the latest generation of Microsoft's operating system, the master program that makes a computer useful and provides support to other programs, including word processors, photo viewers, and web browsers. Much as an education equips you to read a novel or play a game, Windows 8.1 equips your computer to perform a wide range of activities. You can use Windows 8.1 and other software (or *apps*) to read or write a novel, play games or music, and stay in touch with friends and family around the world.

As Windows has evolved over the past 30 years, so have computers — the *hardware*. Today, you can buy a computer as small as a paperback book, and even such a little computer is unimaginably more powerful than (and a fraction of the cost of) computers just 10 years ago. The hardware consists of the screen, as well as optional components such as a keyboard and a mouse.

You don't need much time with a computer to conclude that there has to be an easier way to do things. At times, computers seem overly complex and inscrutable. Have you used a cellphone lately? Or a TV remote control? Why are the controls on every microwave oven different? Why does every new tool offer countless options you don't want that obscure the ones you do want? Well, I don't have the answers to those questions, but I do have step-by-step instructions for many tasks you want to perform using Windows 8.1.

After 35 years working with computers, I find that they reward patience, curiosity, and a little methodical exploration. Seniors, in particular, know that learning never really stops and that learning new things keep one young, at least figuratively. By the end of this book, you may be a multitasking computerist performing virtual gymnastics with Windows 8.1. On the other hand, if this book helps you do only one thing— using e-mail, browsing the Web, or enjoying photos or music— that one useful thing may be all you need.

About This Book

Age is just a number. This book is intended for anyone getting started with Windows 8.1 who wants step-by-step instructions without a lot of discussion. The *Get ready to . . .* bullets at the beginning of each chapter lead you to practical tasks. Numerous figures with notes show you the computer screen as you progress through the steps. Reading this book is like having an experienced friend stand behind you as you use Windows 8.1 . . . someone who never takes control of the computer away from you.

Conventions Used in This Book

This book uses certain conventions to highlight important information and help you find your way around:

➡ **Different methods for performing steps:** In general, you can complete a step in three ways. I list the choices as follows:

- **Mouse:** If you have a mouse, follow these instructions.

- **Touchscreen:** You may be able to touch your screen to perform tasks.

- **Keyboard:** Keyboard shortcuts are often the fastest way to do something.

When you have a choice between these methods, experiment to determine which is easiest for you.

➠ **Tip icons:** Point out helpful suggestions related to tasks in the steps lists.

➠ **Bold:** I use bold for figure references and also when you have to type something onscreen using the keyboard.

 Many figures have notes or other markings to draw your attention to a specific part of the figure. The text tells you what to look for; the figure notes help you find it.

 ➠ **Icons in the margin:** Icons like the one to the left of this text show you what to look for onscreen. It's smaller on your computer screen, so it's blown up here.

➠ **Website addresses:** If you bought an e-book, website address are live links. In the text, website addresses look like this: www.dummies.com. See Chapter 6 for information on browsing the Web.

➠ **Options and buttons:** Although Windows 8.1 often uses lowercase in options and on buttons, I capitalize the text for emphasis. That way, you can find a button labeled Save Now, even though onscreen it appears as *Save now*.

What You're Not to Read

You can work through this book from beginning to end or simply look at the table of contents and find the instructions you need to solve a problem or help you learn a new skill whenever you need it. The steps in each task get you where you want to go quickly without a lot of technical explanation. In no time, you'll start picking up the skills you need to become a confident Windows 8.1 user.

Technology always comes with its own terms and concepts, but you don't need to learn another language to use a computer. You don't need any prior experience with computers or Windows. Step-by-step instructions guide you through specific tasks, such as accessing the news or playing a game. These steps provide just the information you need for the task at hand.

Foolish Assumptions

I assume that you have a computer and want clear, brief, step-by-step instructions on getting things done with Windows 8.1. I assume also that you want to know just what you need to know, just when you need to know it. This isn't Computers 101. This is Practical Windows 8.1. As an old friend of mine said, "I don't want to make a watch; I just want to know what time it is."

How This Book Is Organized

This book is divided into four parts to help you find what you need. You can read from cover to cover or just jump to the page that interests you.

➡ **Part I: Getting Started with Windows 8.1.** In Chapter 1, you turn on the computer and get comfortable with essential parts of Windows 8.1, such as the Start screen, as well as how to use a mouse, touchscreen, or keyboard. Explore features of Windows 8.1 apps in Chapter 2. To customize Windows 8.1 to work better for you, turn to Chapter 3. In Chapter 4, you create and modify user accounts settings, such as passwords. Discover the desktop, a workspace for running apps created before Windows 8.1, in Chapter 5.

➡ **Part II: Windows 8.1 and the Web.** Use the Web to stay current and keep in touch. Turn to Chapter 6 to use Microsoft Internet Explorer to browse the Web. Send and receive e-mail in Chapter 7. Want to stay in touch with family and friends using such popular services as Facebook? See Chapter 8.

➠ **Part III: Having Fun with Windows 8.1.** If you haven't been having any fun until now, I've failed you. Expand your tools and toys in Chapter 9 by connecting to the Microsoft Store to install new apps. In Chapter 10, you enjoy photos on Windows 8.1 and put your own photos on the computer. If you want to listen to music or watch a movie, see Chapter 11.

➠ **Part IV: Beyond the Basics.** In Chapter 12, you learn about the care and feeding of Windows 8.1, which requires a little maintenance now and then. Find out how to connect a printer and other hardware, such as a mouse and a second screen, in Chapter 13. Do you think "a place for everything and everything in its place"? Chapter 14 is where you organize your documents. You back up your files to insure against loss and refresh Windows 8.1 when it gets cranky, all in Chapter 15.

Beyond the Book

A few Windows 8.1 topics I wanted to cover didn't make it into this book. I just didn't have room for them, so I made room elsewhere. By going to the Cheat Sheet and my Website, you can continue your adventures in Windows 8.1:

➠ **Cheat Sheet:** You can find a Cheat Sheet — quick instructions for doing important tasks — at this web address: `www.dummies.com/cheatsheet/windows8dot1forseniors`. The Cheat Sheet tells you how to get to the Start screen, how to go here and there with the App Switcher and Charms bar, and how to switch between open apps and programs. Because passwords can be complicated in Windows 8.1 — What's the difference between a Microsoft account and local password, anyway? — you also find a thorough discussion of handling passwords.

➡ **Updates:** Sometimes Microsoft makes a change to Windows 8.1 without telling me. Imagine that. If Microsoft makes a change that affects material in this book, I wrote about it at this website: www.dummies.com.

Where to Go from Here

Scan the table of contents or the index for a topic that interests you most. Or just turn the page and start at the beginning. It's your book.

Comments and suggestions are welcome. Write me at mark@mjhinton.com.

Part I
Getting Started with Windows 8.1

 Visit www.dummies.com for more great content online.

Getting in Touch with Windows 8.1

Chapter 1

With Windows 8.1, Microsoft created a grand version of Windows, its flagship *operating system* (the master program for any computer). You can use Windows 8.1 on a wide range of devices, from a smartphone to a big-screen TV entertainment system: One size fits most. You can not only use the same programs with a range of hardware but also access the documents you create (such as photos and e-mail — files and data, to nerds) from any Windows-based computer, giving you extraordinary freedom of choice and mobility.

Although countless companies create programs you may use, Microsoft attempts to make similar functions consistent across different programs. For example, opening a document or e-mailing a photo to a friend involves the same steps regardless of the programs you use. You don't have to learn a different way of doing common tasks in each program. This consistency will serve you well when using Windows 8.1 and other new programs.

In this chapter, you start your computer and work with the *Start screen*, the dashboard for Windows 8.1. You explore options for using the Start screen with your *hardware* (the computer and related devices). Then you exit Windows 8.1 and go right back in for more.

For those readers familiar with a previous version of Windows, note that the Start button and menu have been replaced by the new Start button and new Start screen, and the desktop and taskbar are in a new location. See Chapter 5 for more information about the desktop.

 The easiest way to get Windows 8.1 is preinstalled on a new computer. If your current computer runs Windows 7, you can upgrade to Windows 8.1, although an older machine may lack newer functions, such as a touchscreen.

Tell Your Computer What to Do

How do you get Windows 8.1 to do what you want it to do? You can command a computer in many ways, depending on your equipment (hardware). For example, a desktop computer has different options from a handheld phone. You may have any or all of these choices:

➡ **Mouse**

➡ **Touchscreen**

➡ **Keyboard**

Another device for controlling Windows is a touchpad, which is commonly found on a laptop keyboard. You move your finger on the touchpad to move the pointer on the screen. You may also be able to control Windows using speech and a microphone. Microsoft Kinect is a device that enables you to control your computer with a wave of your hand. Welcome to the future!

If you have a computer with more than one of these devices, you might use one device exclusively or, more likely, vary your choice according to the task. Use whichever technique is easiest for you, but don't be afraid to experiment. In the next few sections, you discover the ins and outs of using all these methods of controlling Windows 8.1. Then you're ready to turn on your computer and use these methods.

 In the steps throughout this book, *choose* or *select* refers to using a mouse, the touchscreen, or a physical keyboard. *Drag* refers to using a mouse or a finger.

Move the Mouse

For many years, computers have had a mouse, which is a soap-bar-sized device that you move across a desk with your hand. Move the mouse and note how the arrow called a *mouse pointer* moves across the computer screen. A mouse has two or more buttons; some also have a scroll wheel between the buttons.

The following terms describe methods for using a mouse with Windows 8.1. In each, move the mouse first to position the pointer over a specified item before proceeding:

➡ **Click:** Move the on-screen arrow-shaped mouse pointer over a specified item and press and release the left mouse button: that's a click (sometimes called a left-click to distinguish it from a right-click).

➡ **Right-click:** Press and release the right mouse button to display available functions. Note that the word *click* by itself means use the left mouse button.

➡ **Drag:** Press and hold down the left mouse button, and then move the mouse pointer across the screen. When you want to move an object, you drag it. Release the mouse button to release the object.

 Watch for the word *click* to indicate using a mouse button and *roll* to indicate using the mouse wheel.

Touch the Screen

A *touchscreen*, as the name says, enables you to touch the screen to tell your computer what to do. You typically use one finger or two, although touchscreens may allow you to use all ten digits. In some cases, you can also use a special pen called a *stylus* instead of your finger. Tablet computers and some smartphones have touchscreens. Touchscreens are less common on desktop or laptop computers, but that situation is changing. Not sure what type of screen you have? When you have Windows 8.1 running, give the screen a poke with your index finger to see what happens.

The following terms refer to ways you interact with a touchscreen:

➡ **Tap:** Briefly touch the screen. You *select* an object, such as a button, by tapping it.

➡ **Drag:** Touch and hold your finger on the screen, then move your finger across the screen. You *move* an object, such as an onscreen playing card, by dragging it.

➡ **Swipe:** Touch and move your finger more quickly than with drag. You can swipe your finger across the screen from any of the four sides of the screen to display options and commands. You swipe pages to move forward or back. You may see the word *flick* instead of *swipe*. Some people insist that a flick is faster or shorter than a swipe, but let's not get caught up in that.

➡ **Pinch and unpinch:** Touch a finger and thumb or two fingers on the screen. Move your fingers closer to each other to *pinch* and away from each other to *unpinch*. Generally, a pinch reduces the size of something on the screen or shows more content on the screen. An unpinch (an ugly word) *zooms in*, increasing the size of something on-screen to show more detail.

Watch for the words *tap, swipe,* or *pinch* to indicate using your finger. Touch actions are often called *gestures*.

 See the section "View the Virtual Keyboard" if your computer doesn't have a physical keyboard, as is often the case with a touchscreen.

Use a Keyboard

A typewriter-like keyboard is a traditional device for controlling a computer and is especially useful when you must enter a lot of text. Special key combinations, called *shortcut keys,* are often the quickest way to do anything (though they require some memorization).

The following keys are particularly noteworthy. No offense intended to fans of keys not noted here. Although you won't use all these keys immediately, locate each one on your keyboard.

 Press indicates use the keyboard (physical or virtual) for the specified key or sequence of keys (just as *click* indicates a mouse action and *tap* indicates touch). Combinations of keys are not pressed simultaneously. Instead, press and hold the first key in the specified sequence, press the second key, then release both. (I explain exceptions to this method as necessary.)

➡ ■: Called the Windows key, this key is usually located on either side of the spacebar, which is the largest key. ■ works by itself, as you'll soon see, and also in combination with many other keys. Throughout the book, I specify these combinations where you might use them. There will be a quiz later. (Kidding! No quizzes.)

➡ **Tab:** Press the Tab key to highlight an item. Press Tab repeatedly to skip items you don't intend to select.

The keyboard can be used to select objects but is less direct than using touch or a mouse.

➡ **Arrow keys:** Press the arrow keys to move the cursor or selection of an object in the direction the keys point (left, right, up, or down). In some contexts, Tab and the right arrow do the same thing. Sorry to be vague, but context matters, at times.

➡ **Enter:** In most cases, the Enter key on the keyboard chooses a selection, much as clicking or tapping do. However, you may need to use the Tab key or an arrow key to select an item before pressing the Enter key.

➡ **Ctrl, Alt,** and **Shift keys:** These keys are used with other keys for commands. For example, press Ctrl+C to copy selected text or an object. (That is, while pressing and holding down the Ctrl key, press the C key — no need to press Shift for an uppercase C. Then release both keys.) The Shift key is used with another key for uppercase.

➡ **Backspace:** As you enter text, each press of Backspace erases the character to the left of the cursor.

➡ **Delete:** As you enter text, each press of the Delete key erases the character to the right of the cursor. On some keyboards, this key is labeled Del.

➡ **Function keys:** All keys function, but Function keys are labeled F1 through F12. You don't use these much in this book, but locate them. Laptops often have a separate Function Lock key to turn these keys on or off.

➠ **Page keys:** Locate the Home, End, Page Up, and Page Down keys for future reference. Use these to move the screen, a page, or the cursor.

View the Virtual Keyboard

Windows 8.1 can display a virtual keyboard on-screen. This feature is vital for devices that have a touchscreen and no physical keyboard. With a touchscreen, the virtual keyboard appears automatically when the *cursor* (a blinking vertical bar) indicates that you can enter text in a box. If the virtual keyboard doesn't appear automatically, you may also see a separate box floating above or below the text box. Tap that floating box to display the keyboard. To type using the keyboard, simply tap or click a letter, number, or symbol key.

Different types of virtual keyboards:

➠ The *standard layout* (also called QWERTY) appears automatically (see **Figure 1-1**). The Enter key changes depending on the context.

Standard layout

Figure 1-1

➠ The *uppercase layout,* shown in **Figure 1-2**, appears when you tap the Shift key on the standard layout.

Uppercase layout

Figure 1-2

➠ The *numbers and symbols layout,* shown in **Figure 1-3**, appears when you tap the &123 key on the standard layout. Tap the &123 key again to return to the standard layout.

Numbers and symbols layout

Figure 1-3

➠ The control keys overlay (see **Figure 1-4**) appears on five keys on the standard layout when you tap the Ctrl key. The Ctrl keys are used in common tasks, such as copying (Ctrl+C) or moving (Ctrl+X) selected text. The overlay disappears automatically after you tap one of the control keys (A, Z, X, C, or V).

Ctrl keys layout

Figure 1-4

➠ The *smiley layout,* shown in **Figure 1-5,** appears when you tap the smiley face key. Tap the smiley face key again to return to the standard layout. (Smileys are also called *emoticons* or *emoji.*)

Smiley Keys layout

Figure 1-5

But wait! There's more. Tap the layout key, which is in the lower-right corner of any layout, to display the four options shown in **Figure 1-6.**

Standard

Split

Handwriting

Hide

Layout key

Figure 1-6

➧ Tap the standard button (shown in **Figure 1-6**) to return to the standard layout from the split or handwriting layout. (More on those two layouts next.)

➧ Tap the split button to view the *split keyboard layout,* shown in **Figure 1-7.** This layout is handy for typing with your thumbs while holding two sides of a tablet.

Figure 1-7

➧ Tap the handwriting button to view the *handwriting layout,* shown in **Figure 1-8.** This layout enables you to write with a finger or a stylus (a special pen). Printing usually works better than script.

Handwriting layout

Figure 1-8

If your touchscreen doesn't come with a stylus, you can buy one and use it instead of your finger for improved precision.

➡ Tap the last button to dismiss or hide the virtual keyboard.

Turn On Your Computer

1. Push the power button briefly and release it. Every computer has a power button. (When we can no longer turn them off, the machines win.) If you have a desktop computer tower, the power button is probably on the front of the tower. Otherwise, you might have to feel around the front and sides of the screen or near the hinges of a laptop. Typically, your computer will beep, some buttons will light, and the screen may flash a logo or a message that disappears before you can read it. (Just let that go.) Soon, you will see the first Windows 8.1 screen.

2. Turn on any separate hardware (such as a monitor or a printer).

 The remaining steps in this section occur only when your computer is set up for the first time.

3. The first time you turn on your computer, a series of Windows Setup screens appear. On the initial screen, you select Language to Install, the Time and Currency Format, and the Keyboard or Input Method. Accept the defaults or change them appropriately, and then select the button labeled Next.

4. Select Install Now. (Note the option to Repair Your Computer, used if something goes wrong in the future.) The screen displays *Setup is starting*.

5. If you see a message asking you for a *product key* (a mix of 25 letters and numbers found on the back or bottom of your computer or on related paperwork), type those characters (hyphens are inserted automatically) and then select Next.

 If your computer doesn't have a keyboard, as is the case with many tablet computers, see the preceding section "View the Virtual Keyboard" for information on how to type on-screen.

6. On the License Terms screen, select the check box next to I Accept the License Terms. Feel free to be the first person ever to read the terms before agreeing to them. (If you refuse to accept the terms, you can't use Windows 8.1.) Then select the Next. You may see an indication of the Windows 8.1 installation progress. Your computer may restart during this process, as well.

7. On the Personalize screen, select a background color for the most common screens. When you make a selection, the screen background changes to reflect your choice. Preview as many choices as you like.

8. In the box under PC Name, type a short, simple name for your computer but don't use spaces. The name can be based on location (such as *office*) or computer brand (such as *Dell*) or something more creative (*Firefly* perhaps). This name is visible on a network, if you have one. Select Next.

 You can return to a previous screen (perhaps to confirm or change a selection) by selecting the Back button (an arrow in a circle, near the top-left corner of the screen). The Next button will move you forward again.

9. If a wireless Internet connection is available, you are prompted to select a connection and then enter the network password. For now, select Connect to a Wireless Network Later. See Chapter 4 for information on connecting to a network.

10. On the Settings screen, select the Use Express Settings button for the easiest setup. If you choose the Customize button instead, you'll have to work through several screens of options.

 If this is the first time that Windows 8.1 has started on your computer, you must create a user account, even if no one else will use the machine. See Chapter 4 for details on creating and changing user accounts.

11. If you have an Internet connection, you see the Sign In to Your PC screen. (If you don't have an Internet connection, skip this step.) If you see the Sign in Without a Microsoft Account option, select it. You see a screen summarizing the differences between a Microsoft account and a local account. Select the Local Account button. (You use a Microsoft account in Chapter 4.)

12. In the User Name box, which is shown in **Figure 1-9**, type a short and simple name. Your user name appears throughout the system, from the log-in screen to the Start screen to the location containing all your documents. Use a simple, clear name. Your first name is just fine.

13. In the Password box, type a password. A password is an optional security measure. If you enter a password when you create your user account, that password is required each time you start the computer. If someone other than you tries to start your computer, he or she will have to know (or guess) the password to get into your files. (Don't put your password on a note stuck to the computer or nearby.)

Enter text in these boxes

⟳ Sign in to your PC

If you want a password, choose something that will be easy for you to remember but hard for others to guess.

User name | Example: John |

Password | |

Reenter password | |

Password hint | |

Finish

Figure 1-9

For home computers, passwords may be unnecessary unless you need to keep someone else in the house out of your business. Laptop users should always create a password, however, because it is easy to lose a laptop — don't make it easy for a thief to use your computer.

14. In the Reenter Password box, type the same password again.

15. In the Password Hint box, type a hint to remind yourself — and no one else — what your password is. Do not type the password itself here, or a hint such as *my first name.*

I use my phone number as the hint. That way, if my computer is lost, someone might see my phone number and contact me. (I'm an optimist.)

16. Select the Finish button. The screen may briefly display *Finalizing your settings.* An animation demonstrates that you can move your mouse to any corner or, if you have a touchscreen, swipe from any edge. That's just the tip of the iceberg. The color of the screen and the text on-screen changes a few times to keep you mesmerized as setup finishes. Your PC will be ready in just a moment. Prepare to be awed. Behold, the Windows 8.1 Start screen, shown in **Figure 1-10.** (Your screen may be different than the one in this figure and those throughout the book.)

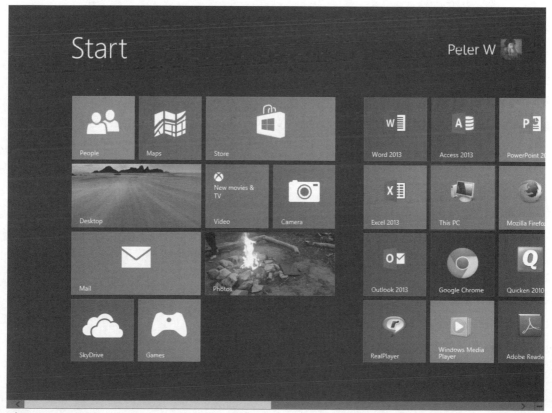

Figure 1-10

Check Out the Start Screen

1. Start your computer — if it isn't started already — and sign in to your user account. You'll see the Start screen, with your user name in the upper-right corner.

2. Examine the Start screen and note the colorful rectangular icons called *tiles.* These tiles represent available *apps* (short for application programs, an older term for programs or software). After you start to use the app tiles, they may display changing information, such as the current weather. (See Chapter 2 for information on using individual apps.)

3. Some tiles may extend beyond the right edge of the screen, (refer to **Figure 1-10**). To see the tiles that are off to the right, use one of the following methods to *scroll* (or move) the screen:

- **Mouse:** Move the mouse pointer to the right edge of the screen, far enough to see the screen move from right to left. You don't use any mouse buttons for this action. Move the mouse pointer to the left edge of the screen to scroll left. You can also roll the mouse wheel toward you to scroll right and away from you to scroll left.

- **Touchscreen:** Tap and hold down a finger in the area below the tiles. Drag from right to left. To scroll back, drag from left to right.

- **Keyboard:** Press the Page Down key to scroll right. Press the Page Up key to scroll left.

4. Use one of the following methods to display the charms bar (see **Figure 1-11**), which provides access to frequently used functions:

- **Mouse:** Move the mouse pointer to the upper-right or lower-right corner of the screen. Then move the mouse pointer out of the corner just a little to transform the charms bar from semitransparent to solid.

- **Touchscreen:** Swipe from the right edge of the screen to reveal the charms bar.

- **Keyboard:** Press ■+C. (Press and hold down the ■ key, press the C key, and then release both keys.)

Start charm

Charms bar

Figure 1-11

When the charms bar is visible, you'll see the time, day, and date in the lower left of the screen and an icon indicating whether your computer is connected to a network.

 See Chapter 5 for information on setting the time.

5. Take a moment to observe the following charms:

- **Search:** Locate apps, documents, and more.

- **Share:** Send photos and more to family and friends.

- **Start:** Display the Start screen, which is useful if you aren't already there, which you are.

- **Devices:** Connect to printers and other devices such as flash drives and hard drives. See Chapter 13 for information on connecting and using a printer.

- **Settings:** Change the look and behavior of Windows 8.1 and individual apps.

 The charms bar gives you quick access to functions used in nearly every app.

6. You'll use all the charms eventually. For now, dismiss the charms bar using one of these methods:

- **Mouse:** Move the mouse pointer away from the charms bar or click the Start charm.

- **Touchscreen:** Tap the Start charm.

- **Keyboard:** Press ■+C.

Shut Down Your Computer

1. When you have finished using your computer for a while, you may want to shut down Windows 8.1. Begin by displaying the charms bar using one of these methods:

- **Mouse:** Move the mouse pointer to the upper-right or lower-right corner of the screen. (The charms bar appears semitransparent.) Then move the mouse pointer out of the corner just a little, until the charms bar becomes solid.

- **Touchscreen:** Swipe from the right edge of the screen to reveal the charms bar.

- **Keyboard:** Press ⊞+C.

2. Select the Settings charm, which is at the bottom of the charms bar (refer to **Figure 1-11**).

3. In the Settings panel, select the Power button. Available options will appear in a pop-up box, as shown in **Figure 1-12**. Some or all of the following options appear:

- **Shut Down:** This option exits Windows 8.1 and saves power by turning the computer off. In exiting Windows 8.1, Shut Down closes any apps that are currently running.

- **Sleep:** This option reduces the computer's power consumption without exiting Windows 8.1 or closing apps. As a result, when you wake the computer by moving the mouse or touching the screen or the keyboard, everything is exactly as you left it: apps and documents are open, if they were before Sleep.

- **Hibernate:** This option combines Sleep and Shut Down. Hibernate records which apps are running but also completely shuts down the computer. When you start the computer, Windows 8.1 opens all programs you were using, just like Sleep.

 Hibernate and Shut Down are equally green options — they save the same amount of power. Sleep is a little less green but saves time if you are returning to the middle of a task.

- **Restart:** Temporarily shuts down Windows 8.1 and turns it on again. Use Restart when Windows 8.1 asks you to or when Windows 8.1 is misbehaving.

Select Power to see available options

Figure 1-12

 You can also shut down your computer using the Start button. Move the pointer to the lower-left corner of the screen. When the Start button appears, select Shut Down or Sign Out on the pop-up menu, and then select an option (Sleep, Shut Down, Hibernate, or Restart).

4. Choose Shut Down to turn off the computer.

 On most computers, pressing the power switch also shuts down the computer. On a laptop, closing the lid may shut down the laptop or put it in sleep or hibernation mode.

For a desktop computer, consider using a power strip to plug in the computer, the monitor, and the printer. After you shut down or hibernate the computer, turn off the power strip to save power.

Start Again on the Lock Screen

1. Turn on your computer. Every time you turn on your computer, the Lock screen appears, displaying the time, day, and date above a photo. (You discover how to change this photo in Chapter 3.) In **Figure 1-13,** note the *badge*, which is a small icon displaying bits of info about networking or an e-mail.

Badge   Lock screen

Figure 1-13

2. Dismiss the Lock screen with one of these methods:

- **Mouse:** Click anywhere, roll the wheel toward you, or drag the entire screen up.

- **Touchscreen:** Drag the entire screen up.

- **Keyboard:** Press any key.

3. If you don't use a password, wait briefly for the Start screen to appear. If you use a password, enter it with a physical or virtual keyboard. Then press Enter or select the arrow next to the password box to display the Start screen.

4. Take a break before reading Chapter 2.

Using the Start Screen and Apps

Chapter 2

*T*he Windows 8.1 *Start screen* provides access to everything you do with Windows 8.1. It's the screen you will see most often and the first screen you see after signing in on the Lock screen. (See Chapter 1 for information on signing in.)

The Start screen is home to numerous programs, or *apps* (short for applications). An app performs a function or displays information. For example, the Weather app displays a local weather report (surprise!) and the Travel app lets you check on a flight and plan a trip. Apps can be simple or more complex, such as the Finance app for stock tracking.

Apps appear on the Start screen as *tiles*. A tile, which may be square or rectangular, displays the app's name and symbol or icon. A tile that displays changing information is called a *live tile*. An open app typically fills the entire screen, hiding everything else. However, some apps can be displayed side-by-side with a function called *snap*.

Get ready to . . .

Two categories of apps are available:

➡ *Windows 8.1 apps* open full screen. In general, Windows 8.1 apps are modern looking and rich with information. They are designed to work with touch-screens as well as with a mouse. Weather and Travel are the first two such apps you use in this chapter. (The News, Sports, and Finance apps function similarly to the Travel app, each with a unique focus.)

➡ *Desktop apps* always open with the desktop behind them. The *desktop* is a holdover from earlier versions of Windows. The desktop enables older programs to work with Windows 8.1. Most desktop apps don't have the look or consistent functions of Windows 8.1 apps. Desktop apps may not respond to touch as reliably as Windows 8.1 apps.

 Apps require a minimum *screen resolution*, which determines how much information the screen can display. Screen resolution is measured in *pixels*, or picture elements. Windows 8.1 requires a screen resolution no less than 1024 pixels wide by 768 pixels high. If your new Windows 8.1 computer has a higher screen resolution, you'll see more information — more tiles and more text — on the screen.

You select an app to use in one of two ways:

➡ **Mouse:** Move the mouse pointer over an app tile. Click the left mouse button to select the tile and open the app.

➡ **Touchscreen:** Tap the app tile with one of your fingers.

In this chapter, you open, close, and use some of the apps that come with Windows 8.1. You also switch between apps and the Start screen and switch directly between two apps. You find out how to search for apps not shown on the Start screen. Finally, you discover how to organize the Start screen by rearranging tiles.

See Chapter 9 for information on getting new apps from the Windows Store.

 Although some steps are specific to one app, most of the steps you follow in this chapter can be repeated in any app.

Open the Weather and Travel Apps

1. On the Start screen, which is shown in **Figure 2-1,** use a mouse or finger to select the tile labeled Weather. The Weather app's *splash screen* appears briefly with the app name.

Weather tile

Figure 2-1

2. The Weather app can determine your location from your network and automatically update your location if you travel with your computer from one city to another. If you see a screen asking *Can Weather Use Your Location?*, select Allow to let the app determine your location; select Block if you want to manually enter the location later.

3. Switch back to the Start screen using one of these methods:

- **Mouse:** Move the mouse pointer to the lower-left corner of the screen. The Start button appears, as shown in **Figure 2-2**. Click the left mouse button.

- **Touchscreen:** Swipe a finger from the right edge of the screen to display the charms bar. (For more on the charms bar, see Chapter 1.) Tap the Start button in the middle of the charms bar.

- **Keyboard:** Press the ■ key to suspend the Weather app temporarily and switch back to the Start screen.

Start button

Figure 2-2

Focus on the method you think is easiest. However, keep in mind that alternative methods of controlling your computer are always available.

4. On the Start screen, check to see if the Weather tile is displaying current weather information, as in **Figure** 2-3. The Weather app has a *live tile*, which displays changing information for a location (even the wrong location is okay for now). See "Add a Location in Weather" for information on setting your location.

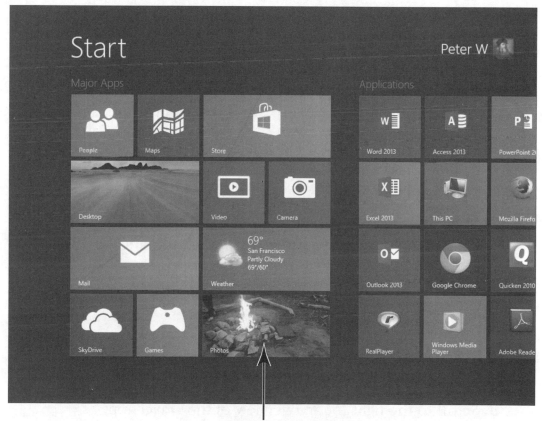

Weather has a live tile

Figure 2-3

5. Switch back to the Weather app by selecting the Weather tile or by using one of the methods in Step 3, which alternate between the Start screen and the most recently open app. The Weather app reappears and takes up the full screen.

6. Switch back to the Start screen.

7. Select the Travel tile (look for a suitcase icon). To see this tile, you may have to move (*scroll*) the screen to the right using one of these methods:

   - **Mouse:** With the mouse pointer anywhere, roll the mouse wheel toward you, or move the mouse pointer to the right edge of the screen without rolling the wheel. Keep moving the mouse to the right to continue scrolling. No mouse buttons are used for this operation. (To scroll left, roll the mouse wheel away from you or move the mouse pointer to the left edge of the screen.)

   - **Touchscreen:** Press a finger below the tiles and drag your finger right to left. Or swipe from right to left, lifting your finger quickly. To scroll left, drag or swipe your finger from left to right.

   - **Keyboard:** Press the Page Down (PgDn) key to scroll to the right. Press Page Up (PgUp) to scroll to the left.

   The Travel splash screen appears briefly. The Travel home screen appears, as shown in **Figure 2-4**.

8. Scroll to the right for an overview of the Travel app, which shows travel destinations, photos, and articles.

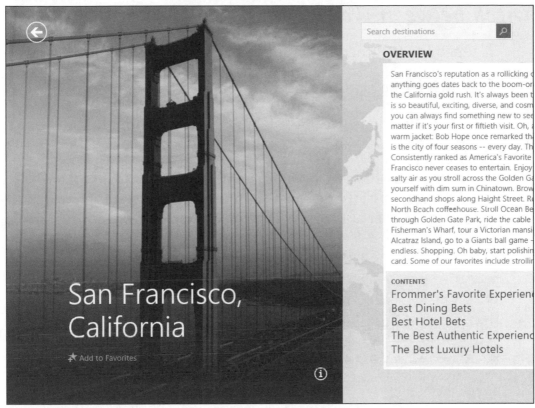

San Francisco,
California

⭐ Add to Favorites

Search destinations

OVERVIEW

San Francisco's reputation as a rollicking
anything goes dates back to the boom-or
the California gold rush. It's always been t
is so beautiful, exciting, diverse, and cosm
you can always find something new to see
matter if it's your first or fiftieth visit. Oh,
warm jacket: Bob Hope once remarked th
is the city of four seasons -- every day. Th
Consistently ranked as America's Favorite
Francisco never ceases to entertain. Enjoy
salty air as you stroll across the Golden Ga
yourself with dim sum in Chinatown. Brow
secondhand shops along Haight Street. R
North Beach coffeehouse. Stroll Ocean Be
through Golden Gate Park, ride the cable
Fisherman's Wharf, tour a Victorian mansi
Alcatraz Island, go to a Giants ball game -
endless. Shopping. Oh baby, start polishin
card. Some of our favorites include strollin

CONTENTS
Frommer's Favorite Experien
Best Dining Bets
Best Hotel Bets
The Best Authentic Experien
The Best Luxury Hotels

Figure 2-4

9. Switch to the Start screen using one of the methods in Step 3. Note that when you switch between Travel (or another app) and the Start screen, the Weather app remains hidden. Note as well that the live Travel tile shows changing destinations.

10. On the Start screen, select the Weather tile. Switch back and forth from the Weather app to the Start screen a few times to get comfortable switching between an app and the Start screen.

Switch between Weather and Travel

1. Open the Weather app as in the preceding section.

2. Switch to the Start screen, and open the Travel app.

3. Switch directly between open apps (without going to the Start screen) by using one of these methods:

- **Mouse:** Move the mouse pointer to the upper-left corner of the screen. A thumbnail preview of the Weather app appears in that corner, as shown in **Figure 2-5**. Click the left mouse button.

Travel thumbnail

Figure 2-5

 If clicking in the left corner doesn't switch to the other app, you may not have two apps open. Or you may have more than two apps open, in which case you must click repeatedly until the desired app is displayed.

- **Touchscreen:** Press and hold down your finger outside the left edge of the screen. Drag your finger to the right and lift your finger when the other app appears. This action is called a *swipe*. It's kinda cool.

- **Keyboard:** Press ⊞+Tab. (In other words, while pressing and holding down the ⊞ key, press the Tab key. Then release both keys quickly.) The *app switcher* appears on the left and then the screen switches to the Weather app. You find out more about this feature next.

Use the App Switcher

1. Start the Weather app, and then start the Travel app.

2. Switch back to the Start screen.

3. Use one of the following methods to display the app switcher (see **Figure 2-6**), which shows thumbnails for open apps, and switch to the Weather app:

- **Mouse:** Place the pointer in the upper-left corner of the screen. Don't click. When a thumbnail appears, move the mouse pointer down until the app switcher appears. Click the Weather thumbnail.

- **Touchscreen:** Slowly swipe from the left edge of the screen, and then swipe back to the left edge without lifting your finger. Tap the Weather thumbnail.

- **Keyboard:** Hold down the key, and press and release the Tab key to display the app switcher. Press Tab until the Weather thumbnail is high-lighted. Then release both keys.

When you quickly press and release both ⊞ and Tab, the app switcher appears briefly. When you instead hold down ⊞ and press and release Tab, the app switcher remains on the screen and you can keep pressing Tab to select different thumb-nails. Release ⊞ to switch to the highlighted app. If you press ⊞+Ctrl+Tab — a test of your dexter-ity — the app switcher stays on-screen without you having to hold down any keys. Then you can press Tab to select the thumbnail you want and Enter or the space bar to switch to that app. (That may be more than you wanted to know, but it's literally handy.)

App switcher

Figure 2-6

 In **Figure 2-6**, thumbnails appear for Weather and Travel apps. You may notice the Start button at the bottom of the app switcher. No thumbnail appears for the app you are using when you display the app switcher.

 You can switch between two apps without seeing the app switcher, as detailed in the preceding section. The app switcher comes in handy when you want to see thumbnails for several open apps at once.

Snap Two (or More) Apps to Display Them

1. From the Start screen, open the Weather and Travel apps, if they're not already open. (Refer to the "Open the Weather and Travel Apps" section.) Switch to the Travel app.

2. Use one of these techniques to *snap* (position) the Weather app next to the Travel app, as shown in **Figure 2-7**.

- **Mouse:** Place the mouse pointer in the upper-left corner of the screen. Hold down the left mouse button and drag the Weather thumbnail down until the screen splits into a narrow pane on the left for the Weather app and a wider pane on the right for Travel. Release the mouse button.

- **Touchscreen:** Swipe (press your finger down and drag) from beyond the left edge of the screen to the right. When the Weather app thumbnail appears, drag just far enough to see the screen split. A quick swipe from the left replaces one app with another. A slow swipe splits the screen.

- **Keyboard:** Press ⊞ and the period key to snap the current app to one side. Press ⊞+period (.) again to snap to the other side. Use the app switcher to position the other app in the larger area of the screen. Press ⊞+period a third time to restore one app to full screen. You can continue repeating this sequence until you find the screen arrangement you prefer.

Divider   Dots

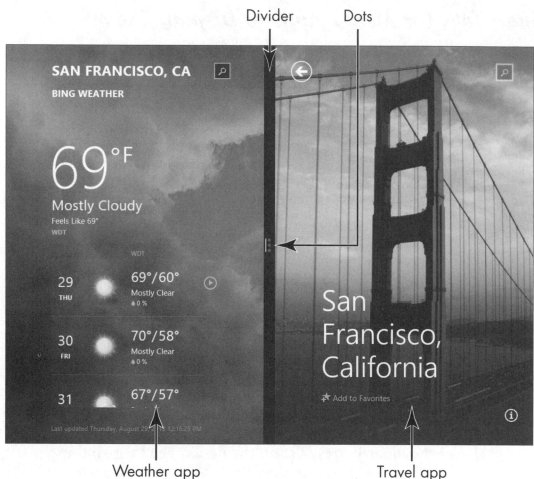

Weather app   Travel app

Figure 2-7

 In the preceding section, you dragged an app far
enough toward the middle of the screen to replace
another app. To snap, don't drag the second app too
far from the edge of the screen. Watch for the screen
to split.

 If you can't get the two apps side-by-side, the problem may be your screen resolution, not you. The
minimum screen resolution for side-by-side app display is 1366 pixels (dots) wide by 768 pixels high. If
you can't complete these steps, your screen may not
support this feature.

3. Give the Weather app the larger share of the screen by dragging the bar between the two apps or double-clicking (double-tapping) the three dots in the middle of the bar that separates the two panes (refer to **Figure 2-7**). The two windows are restricted in size, roughly 25 percent to 75 percent, as shown in **Figure 2-8.** You can't choose sizes in between.

 Apps may show different information or functions when snapped to the smaller pane. For example, when Weather is in the smaller pane, only the next few days are forecast.

Reproportioned windows

Figure 2-8

You can snap more than two apps to the screen. To do so, use the same techniques you use to display an additional app onscreen (see Step 2). Whether displaying more than two apps is worthwhile depends on the size of your monitor screen. You need a wide screen to display more than two apps and be able to use them comfortably.

4. Drag the bar between panes all the way left or right to make one app full screen.

5. If the Travel app isn't on-screen already, switch to it by using the app switcher (see the preceding section).

6. Place Weather on the right instead of the left by dragging the Weather app thumbnail to the right side of the screen before letting go. Now Travel is in the wide pane on the left and Weather is in the narrow pane on the right, as shown in **Figure 2-9**. This procedure is different than resizing the two panes, as you did in Step 4 (refer to **Figure 2-7**), because Weather is on the right.

7. Drag the bar between the panes left or right far enough to hide one app, leaving the other full screen.

 To avoid snapping when you don't want two apps on screen at once, use the mouse to drag the incoming app thumbnail far enough to see its left edge. Watch how the screen changes between snap and full screen. Then let go of the thumbnail. With a touch-screen, a quick swipe or *flick* from the left replaces one app with another. A slow swipe splits the screen; to snap, let go when you see that split.

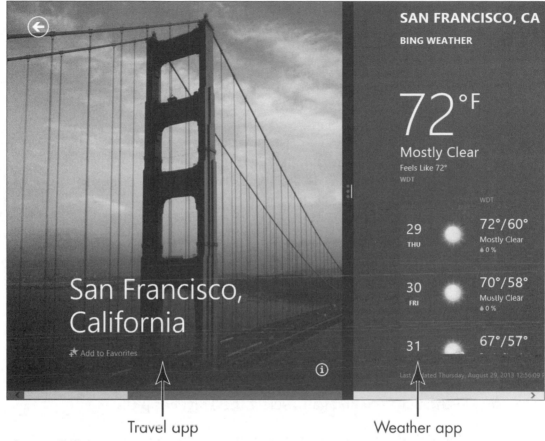

Travel app   Weather app

Figure 2-9

Close the Weather and Travel Apps

1. On the Start screen, select the Weather app tile. Switching to another app or the Start screen hides the Weather app but doesn't *close* it (stop it from running).

2. Close any open app with one of these methods:

- **Mouse:** Move the mouse pointer to the top edge of the screen, where the pointer changes to an open hand (see the margin). Hold down the left mouse button and the hand closes. Drag the app down to the bottom of the window. When part of the app is off the bottom of the screen, the app shrinks to a thumbnail. Let go to close the app.

- **Touchscreen:** Place your finger above the top edge of the screen (off the screen). Swipe down to the bottom of the window. When part of the app is off the bottom of the screen, the app shrinks to a thumbnail. Let go and the app closes.

- **Keyboard**: Press Alt+F4.

 You don't have to close apps. However, having unneeded apps open makes switching between apps more of a challenge because of unneeded thumbnails in the app switcher.

3. On the Start screen again, select the Travel app tile.

4. In Travel, drag down or swipe down until the app shrinks and then let go to close the app. Or press Alt+F4.

 You can use the mouse to close an app by using the app switcher. Position the pointer over a thumbnail and click with the right button. A context menu appears, as shown in **Figure 2-10**. With the left button, click Close. You can also use this menu to snap an app to the screen (Insert Left or Insert Right) or replace an app on the screen.

Use the App Bar

1. From the Start screen, open the Travel app.

Close, replace, or insert an app.

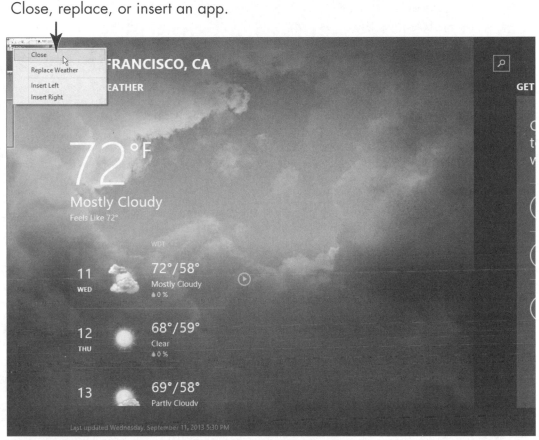

Figure 2-10

2. The *app bar,* shown in **Figure 2-11,** contains functions specific to the current app. Display the app bar by using one of these methods:

- **Mouse:** With the pointer anywhere in the app, right-click (click the right mouse button).

- **Touchscreen:** Swipe down from the top or up from the bottom. Use a short swipe; don't swipe far enough to close the app.

- **Keyboard:** Press ⊞+Z.

App bar

Figure 2-11

 The app bar may appear across the bottom of the screen, the top of the screen, or in both locations.

3. In the Travel app, the app bar leads you to travel-specific functions. Select Destinations on the app bar, which then disappears. On the Destinations screen, scroll to the right for an overview. To refine the scope of your browsing, use the Region option.

4. Display the app bar in Travel again. Then select the Flights or Hotels button. You could use either to book a trip.

5. Display the app bar again. Select the Home button to return to the app *home screen*, which is the screen you see when you start an app for the first time.

You can also use the Back button (an arrow in a circle), which is found in the upper-left corner of many screens, to return to the preceding screen, not necessarily the home screen.

Add a Location in Weather

1. From the Start screen, open the Weather app. With the Weather app on the screen, display the app bar using one of the methods in the preceding section. In **Figure 2-12**, the Weather app bar appears at the top and bottom of the screen.

Figure 2-12

2. Select the Places button at the top of the screen. The Places screen appears, as shown in **Figure 2-13**. Unless you're lucky enough to live in San Francisco, your screen will show a different live tile.

Divider

Figure 2-13

3. Select the Add Place tile, which looks like a plus in a circle. The Enter location screen appears.

4. Type a location name, such as a city, in the box under Enter Location, as shown in **Figure 2-14**. As you type, matching location names appear below the box. If you see the location you want, select that name to add a tile for that location to the Places screen. No need to click the Add button, unless your location does not appear automatically.

You can add other locations by repeating Steps 3 and 4.

Type in the box

Figure 2-14

5. Select the tile for the location you added. The Weather app displays full information for the location you selected.

 You can switch between multiple locations by using the Places button on the app bar.

6. Return to the Start screen. Your new location does not appear — yet. Select the Weather tile, and your added location appears. Display the app bar (see **Figure 2-15**). In addition to the app bar at the top of the screen, an app bar for the selected location appears at the bottom of the screen.

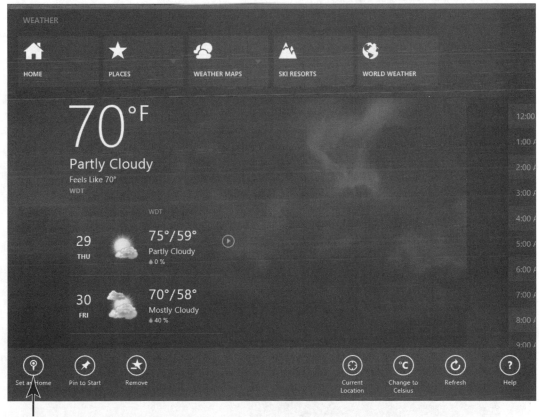

App bar for selected location
Figure 2-15

7. Select the Pin to Start button at the bottom of the screen to add a tile for the current location to the Start screen. (If you don't see Pin to Start, repeat Steps 2–5 to add a location.) You can add a note to the tile by entering text in the box where the location name appears, as shown in **Figure 2-16**. (For example, you might type a person's name if you display the weather where that person lives.) Then select the Pin to Start button.

Type here

Figure 2-16

8. Return to the Start screen. The original Weather tile appears, as well as the new tile. You may have to scroll to the right with the mouse or by dragging your finger right to left to see the new Weather tile, as in **Figure 2-17**.

Figure 2-17

9. Select the new Weather tile to open the app with that location.

10. Display the app bar for Weather, which is shown in **Figure 2-18**. Select the Unpin from Start button at the bottom of the screen to remove from the Start screen the tile for the current location. Select Unpin from Start in the pop-up menu. If Unpin from Start doesn't appear, repeat Step 7.

11. Return to the Start screen. The location you unpinned no longer appears.

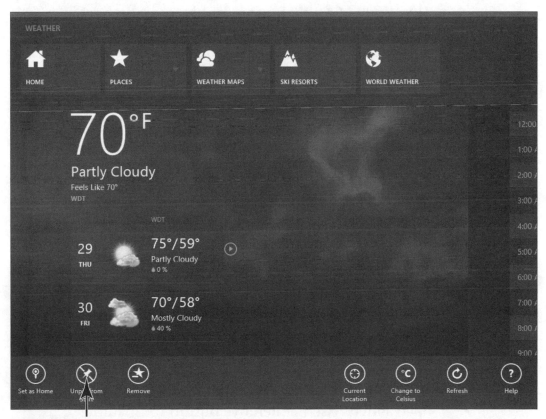

Select the Unpin from Start button

Figure 2-18

Add locations for friends, family, and travel destinations and pin these new locations to the Start screen. See the section "Arrange Apps on the Start Screen" if you want to group these tiles.

12. In the Weather app, several other buttons may appear. See if your screen displays any of the following (refer to **Figure 2-18**):

- The Home button (on the top app bar) displays weather for the *default* (original) location if you are displaying any other location.

- The World Weather button (on the top app bar) is cool. Select it now! A map of the world appears with weather for some locations. Click or tap an area on the map to zoom in for more locations. Select any location to display weather full-screen for that location. (This action does not add the location to your list of places.) Select the Back button if you want to return to the main Weather screen without displaying a new location.

- The Set as Home button (on the bottom app bar) makes the currently displayed location the default location.

- The Add button (on the bottom app bar but not shown in **Figure 2-18**) appears for a location you chose from World Weather. Use the Add button if you want to add the displayed location to the Places screen.

- The Remove button appears for a location you have added. Use the Remove button to unclutter the Places screen.

- The Change to Celsius button switches temperatures to that scale, in which case the button becomes Change to Fahrenheit.

- The Refresh button updates the screen, although that should happen automatically.

Change App Settings

1. On the Start screen, select the Weather tile.

2. In the Weather app, display the charms bar and select the Settings charm using one of the following methods:

- **Mouse:** Move the pointer to the lower-right corner of the screen to display the charms bar. Click the Settings charm.

- **Touchscreen:** Swipe from the right edge toward the left. Tap Settings.

- **Keyboard:** Press ■+I to display the Settings panel without displaying the charms bar first. This short-cut key is hard to beat for quick access to Settings.

 It may be hard to remember whether you need the Settings panel or the app bar to do something. In general, functions on the app bar are used more frequently than those on the Settings panel. When in doubt, guess — that's how discoveries are made.

3. The Settings panel for Weather appears, as shown in **Figure 2-19.** Select each of the following settings in Weather. Use the Back button (the back arrow) to move from each of these back to the main Settings panel.

- The Microsoft Advertising option lets you decide whether Microsoft can direct advertisements to you on the basis of your history using the Weather app.

Figure 2-19

- The Options setting displays a screen that includes Search History, which records searches you make in the Weather app for locations (see the preceding section). The Clear Weather Searches button erases any previous location searches, but not locations you added or pinned. Leave the Search History settings as they are for now.

- The About option displays the app's version number and creator along with additional information.

- Use the Feedback option to provide direct feedback to the app developer, which in this case is Microsoft. See **Figure 2-20**. Your comments may help improve the app.

- The Terms of Use and Privacy Statement options open in the browser web pages with specific legal language regarding the app. In general, you have no rights and they have no liabilities.

- The Privacy Statement option opens a Web page with information about how the app developer (Microsoft in this case) uses your personal information.

- The Help option provides information for using the Weather app.

 The top portion of the Settings panel is specific to the open app. The bottom section contains systemwide settings, covered in Chapters 3 and 4.

 Changes to settings take effect immediately. You don't have to save or activate your changes.

Figure 2-20

Search for a Desktop App

1. On the Start screen, type **calc** (the first four letters of the word *calculator*). The Search panel appears on the right side of the screen, as shown in **Figure 2-21**, with the letters you type in a box in the upper right of the screen. The Search panel below the box lists app names, program names, settings, files, and web pages with the term you entered. You can search for just about anything by typing when the Start screen is displayed.

Search text

Figure 2-21

You can search for more than apps, including settings and files. To use Search in any app, display the charms bar and select the Search charm. For example, search for a city in the Weather or Travel apps.

2. Type **ulator** to finish typing the word *calculator*. The Search panel lists only items with the complete word *calculator* in them, including the Windows 8.1 Calculator program and the Calculator app.

3. Select the Calculator program to open it on the desktop, as shown in **Figure 2-22**. To perform a calculation, select the buttons on the screen or use a keyboard.

Calculator tile   Desktop

Figure 2-22

4. Return to the Start screen: Click the Windows button in the lower-left corner of the desktop, swipe in from the left edge of the screen, or press .

5. Repeat the steps you just used to switch back and forth between the Start screen and the Calculator app on the desktop.

6. Switch to the Start screen.

7. Display the app switcher and switch back to the desktop using one of the following methods:

- **Mouse:** Move the pointer to the upper-left corner to reveal the desktop thumbnail. Move the pointer down the left side of the screen without clicking to display the app switcher. Drag the desktop thumbnail to the right; drag a little to split the screen or more to fill the screen.

- **Touchscreen:** Swipe from the left edge of the screen and back to display the app switcher. Swipe the desktop thumbnail to the right slowly to split the screen or quickly to fill the screen.

- **Keyboard:** Press +Tab until the desktop thumbnail is highlighted, then release both keys.

 You can use two keystrokes to switch to desktop apps. Press Alt+Tab to display thumbnails for open Windows 8.1 apps, open desktop apps, and the desktop itself. Press +D to switch from the Start screen to the desktop. See Chapter 5 for more information on the desktop.

 If your screen resolution allows, you can snap the desktop beside other apps. This procedure works best when the desktop is in the larger part of the screen. Note that you can snap only the entire desktop, not individual desktop apps.

8. Close the entire desktop like any other app, with one of the following methods:

- **Mouse:** Move the mouse pointer to the top center of the desktop until the pointer changes into an open hand. Drag down until part of the desktop is off the screen, and then release the mouse button to close the desktop.

- **Touchscreen:** Swipe down from the top edge until part of the desktop is off the screen.

 These methods close both the Calculator and the desktop. To close only the Calculator, switch to the desktop and click the white X in the red box in the upper-right corner of the Calculator (refer to **Figure 2-22**).

Display All Windows 8.1 Apps

1. The Start screen displays only some of the apps available in Windows 8.1. To see all the apps in Windows 8.1, select the All Apps button (see **Figure 2-23**). This button is on the bottom left of the screen.

2. The Apps screen appears, as shown in **Figure 2-24**. You may have to roll the mouse wheel toward you or drag from right to left to see all the icons. Besides scrolling, you can also use these techniques to locate an app:

- **Sorting:** Open the Sort drop-down menu and select an option to arrange apps by name, by the date they were installed, by most used, or by category.

- **Searching:** Type the name of the app in the Search box in the upper-right corner of the screen.

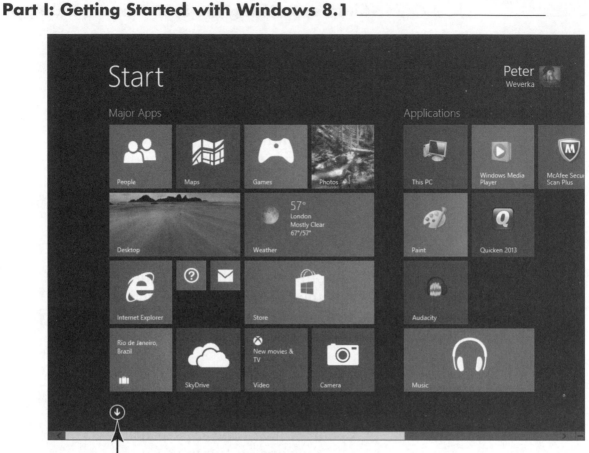

All Apps button

Figure 2-23

3. By scrolling, sorting, or searching, locate the Calculator app. After you locate the app, use one of the following methods to select — but not open — the Calculator tile:

- **Mouse:** Position the pointer over the tile and right-click. (A left click would open the app.)

- **Touchscreen:** Swipe slightly down or up on the tile. (A direct tap would open the app.)

- **Keyboard:** Use the arrow keys to select the app. Then press the context menu key (shown in the margin), which is usually next to the right-hand ⊞ key.

Apps by name ⌄

Alarms	Health & Fitness	Music	SkyDrive
Audacity	Hearts (Free)	News	Skype
Calculator	Help+Tips	PC settings	Sound Recorder
Calendar	Internet Explorer	People	Sports
Camera	Mahjong Deluxe Free	Photo Gallery NEW	Store
Desktop	Mail	Photos	Travel
Finance	Maps	Reader	Video
Food & Drink	Movie Maker	Reading List	WD
Games	Mozilla Firefox	Scan	Weather

Return to Start screen

Figure 2-24

 A check mark next to a tile indicates that the tile is selected.

4. The app bar appears automatically when you select a tile, as shown in **Figure 2-25**. Select Pin to Start to place the Calculator tile on the Start screen. The app bar disappears and you return to the Start screen, where you see the Calculator tile you selected in Step 3.

 To remove an app tile from the Start screen, right-click the tile. The Customize bar appears. Select the Unpin from Start button on the Customize bar. (The programs are not removed when you unpin.)

Place a tile for the app on the Start screen.
Figure 2-25

5. Select the All Apps button (in the bottom left of the screen) to return to the Apps screen.

6. Click the Return to Start screen button to return to the Start screen. This button is located in the lower left portion of the screen. It shows an upward-pointing arrow.

Arrange and Group Apps on the Start Screen

1. You can rearrange tiles on the Start screen by dragging them to different places. On the Start screen, drag the Calculator tile to a different location. As you move the tile, other tiles move out of the way, like a game of Dodge Tile.

2. Create a new group for Calculator by dragging the Calculator tile to the right of all the other tiles. When a vertical bar appears, as shown in **Figure 2-26,** release the Calculator tile. You just created a new group with Calculator as the only tile.

3. It's time to name the new group. Begin by displaying the Customize bar:

- **Mouse:** Right-click anywhere on the screen but on a tile.

- **Touchscreen:** Press and hold anywhere on screen except on a tile.

Figure 2-26

4. Select the Customize button on the App bar. The Start screen dims to indicate that it is in Customization mode.

5. Type a name for the group, as shown in **Figure 2-27**. The new name appears above the group, although the name may appear shortened on this screen. You can change the name at any time by repeating Steps 4 and 5. To remove the name, select the X to the right of the text box.

Enter a group name.

Figure 2-27

6. Use one of the following methods to select — but not open — the Calculator tile:

- **Mouse:** Position the pointer over the tile and right-click. (A left click would open the app.)

- **Touchscreen:** Swipe slightly down or up on the tile. (A direct tap would open the app.)

- **Keyboard:** Use the arrow keys to select the app. Then press the context menu key (shown in the margin), which is usually next to the right-hand ⊞ key.

A check mark next to a tile indicates that the tile is selected.

7. Change the size of the Calculator tile. On the Customize bar, select the Resize button and select the Wide option on the pop-up menu; see **Figure 2-28**. As well as the Wide, Medium, and Small options, Windows 8.1 provides a Large option for some tiles.

 Choose the Large or Wide resize option for apps you use often. The larger the tile, the easier it is to find on the Start screen.

Weather app

Figure 2-28

8. Locate a tile on the Start screen that doesn't need to be there. Then select the tile and select the Unpin from Start button on the app bar. (See Step 6 if you need instructions for selecting a tile on the Start screen.)

 The Start screen becomes more useful and personal when you eliminate tiles you don't need and arrange tiles to suit your sense of order.

9. Click the screen to exit Customization mode.

Adjusting Windows 8.1 PC Settings

Chapter

3

*O*ut of the box, Windows 8.1 is showy and colorful. If you don't like that look, however, you can change the photos and colors you see on the screen. Adjusting Windows 8.1 PC settings can also make Windows 8.1 easier and more fun to use. When you're ready, you can dive in and make Windows 8.1 yours.

In this chapter, you personalize the Lock screen and change the colors and background design on the Start screen. You'll see these screens many times a day, so they should please you. Choose a picture to identify your account. Finally, make your screen easier to see and enable features such as Narrator, which reads aloud content from the screen.

Many people leave Windows 8.1 largely as they found it. Some love to tweak, tinker, and tune. How far you go in personalizing Windows 8.1 is up to you — it's your computer, after all.

See Chapter 4 for information on changing passwords and other user settings.

Access PC Settings

1. On the Start screen, display the charms bar (see **Figure 3-1**) and select Settings with one of these methods:

- **Mouse:** Move the mouse pointer into the lower-right corner of the screen to display the charms bar, and then click Settings.

- **Touchscreen:** Swipe from the right edge of the screen to display the charms bar, and then tap Settings.

- **Keyboard:** Press +I to go straight to Settings, skipping the charms bar.

 You can complete the following steps with a mouse, the keyboard, or a touchscreen. Find the right combination of methods for you. Experiment and play.

2. The Settings panel appears, the bottom portion of which is shown in **Figure 3-2**. Select Change PC Settings by moving the pointer over the item and clicking, or by tapping the item.

 Options near the top of the Settings panel are for the open app, if any.

Settings charm

Figure 3-1

Select to view the PC settings screen

Figure 3-2

3. The PC Settings screen appears, as shown in **Figure** 3-3.
One at a time, select each heading on the left, starting
with PC and Devices, to see the options available. Select
the Back button (the circle with the left-pointing arrow,
located in the upper-left corner of the screen) to return to
the top settings.

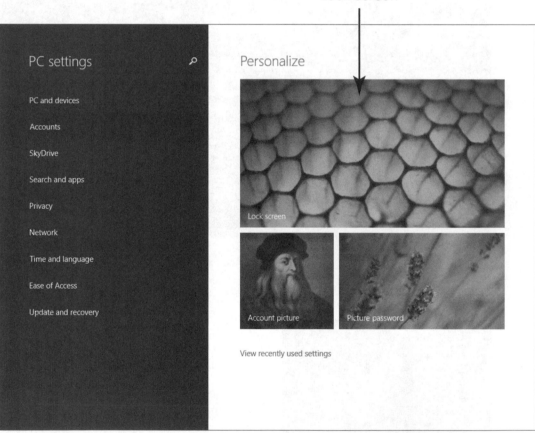

Figure 3-3

Personalize the Lock Screen

1. On the PC Settings screen, select Lock Screen (refer to **Figure 3-3**).

 The Lock screen is the first screen you see when you start Windows 8.1.

2. Just above the Browse button, select each thumbnail photo, one at a time. The larger preview photo above changes and the thumbnails shift to the right, with the previously selected photo taking the first position in the row, as shown in **Figure 3-4**. Select a photo that's different from the one you started with. (You can always change it later.)

Choose a thumbnail

Figure 3-4

You can use the Browse button to select one of your own photos from the Pictures folder. See Chapter 10 for information on adding photos to this folder and its subfolders.

 Rather than see one image on the start screen, you can see a slide show of images in your Pictures folder. On the Lock Screen screen (refer to Figure 3-4), turn on the Play a Slide Show on the Lock Screen option.

3. Return to the Start screen. Select your account name in the upper-right corner to display the menu shown in **Figure 3-5**, and then select Lock to display the Lock screen.

Figure 3-5

 You can lock your computer anytime by pressing ⊞+L.

4. The photo you selected in Step 2 appears on the Lock screen. Display the Password screen as follows:

- **Mouse:** Click anywhere.

- **Touchscreen:** Swipe up.

- **Keyboard:** Press any key on the keyboard.

5. Enter your password, if you have one. The Start screen appears.

Choose an Account Picture

1. On the PC Settings screen, select Account Picture. See "Access PC Settings" for help. Your current Account picture appears in the Accounts screen, as shown in **Figure 3-6**. (If you haven't selected a picture yet, your picture may just be an outline.)

Current account picture

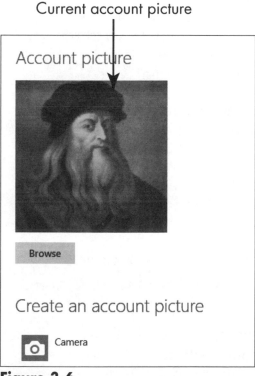

Account picture

Browse

Create an account picture

Camera

Figure 3-6

 Your account picture appears on the Password screen and on the Start screen.

2. To choose one of your photos, select the Browse button. The contents of your Pictures folder appears. From this screen, you can select Go Up to access any folder on your computer or select a subfolder to open. When you find the picture you want, select it and then select the Choose Image button. Or select Cancel to return to the previous screen without changing your account picture.

 See Chapter 10 for information about adding photos to your Pictures folder.

3. If you have a built-in or attached camera (called a *web-cam*), select the Camera app under Create an Account Picture. The Camera app opens with a preview of what your camera sees. If you see Connect a Camera, select the back arrow to the left of Camera. See Chapter 10 for information on taking pictures with a webcam.

 You may be able to use another app to select or create a picture. Select the app under Create an Account Picture (refer to **Figure 3-6**).

4. Return to the Start screen to see your new account picture (mine is shown in **Figure 3-7**) using one of these methods:

- **Mouse:** Click the pointer in the lower-left corner of the screen. Repeat to switch back to the Personalize screen.

- **Touchscreen:** Swipe from the right edge of the screen and then tap the Start button. Repeat to switch back to the Personalize screen.

- **Keyboard:** Press ▦. Repeat to switch back to the Personalize screen.

Click to change your account picture

Peter W

Change account picture

Lock

Sign out

Bobby

Figure 3-7

 The easiest way to access the Accounts screen and change your account picture is through your account name. In the upper-right corner of the Start screen, select your name and then select Change Account Picture (see **Figure 3-7**). Voilà! The Accounts screen appears, with Your Account selected. You don't have to change your picture to use this shortcut.

Check for Important Updates

1. To check for updates to Windows 8.1, select Update and Recovery on the PC Settings screen. See "Access PC Settings" for help getting to the PC Settings screen.

2. On the Update and Recovery screen, select Windows Update. The Windows Update screen appears, as shown in **Figure 3-8**.

 If you don't mind typing, you can get to the Windows Update screen by typing **windows update** on the Start screen and selecting Windows Update settings in the search panel.

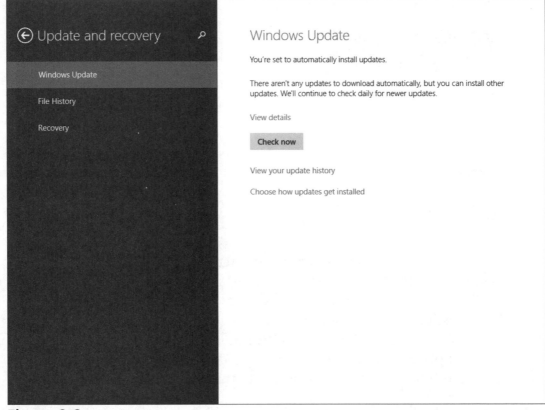

Figure 3-8

3. The Windows Update screen informs you that Windows 8.1 automatically installs important updates, such as security enhancements. You also see when Windows 8.1 last checked for updates and whether any were found. Select the Check Now button to find out if any updates are available and update Windows 8.1 on your computer.

4. You may see a message that one or more updates have been scheduled to be installed. You do not have to do anything to install these updates — the update process is automatic. However, if you select the link to schedule updates, you can see details and select the Install button if you want to. Otherwise, return to the Start screen to let Windows 8.1 manage updates automatically.

Installing an update seldom takes more than a few minutes. You can use your system during the update process. If the update process requires that you restart your computer, you will see a message on the Windows Update screen and the Lock screen. If you don't restart when required, Windows 8.1 will automatically restart within two days of the first notification.

 For information on other updates and maintaining Windows 8.1, see Chapter 12.

Make Windows 8.1 Easier to Use

1. On the PC Settings screen, select Ease of Access, as shown in **Figure** 3-9. (See "Access PC Settings" for help.) The Ease of Access screens offer many ways to make your computer, mouse, and monitor easier to use.

Figure 3-9

2. Choose Narrator settings (refer to **Figure** 3-9) to have content on the screen read aloud. These settings are for people who have difficulty reading. After turning on the Narrator switch, you choose voice, speed, and pitch settings to determine what the narrator's voice sounds like.

3. Choose Magnifier settings to enlarge what is on your computer screen. These settings are for people who have difficulty seeing. When Magnifier is turned on, the Magnifier toolbar appears onscreen. (Click the magnifying glass icon to see this toolbar, if necessary.) Click the plus sign on the Magnifier toolbar to zoom a portion of the screen for easier viewing, as shown in **Figure** 3-10. Click the minus sign to see the screen at normal size.

 Without turning the Magnifier switch on, you can magnify the screen. Press ⊞+plus key to zoom in using Magnifier. Press ⊞+minus key to zoom out using Magnifier.

4. Choose High Contrast settings to alter the screen in a way that might make it easier to see text. These settings are also for people who have difficulty seeing. After you choose a theme, you can choose a color for text, hyperlinks, disabled text, selected text, button text, and backgrounds. Click Apply after you make your choices. Choose None and click Apply if you want to return to the default Windows 8.1 contrast settings.

5. Choose Keyboard settings to type without using a physical keyboard. This onscreen keyboard uses the layout of a conventional keyboard. However, most people find that the standard Windows 8.1 virtual keyboard is more flexible. See Chapter 1 for information on the virtual keyboard layouts.

6. Choose Mouse settings to change the size and color of the mouse pointer. As shown in **Figure** 3-11, Windows 8.1 offers mouse pointers of different sizes and colors. Choose the combination that tickles your fancy.

Magnify things on the screen

Magnifier

On

Invert colors

Off

Start Magnifier automatically

On

Magnifier   —   □   ×

200%   Views ▼

Tracking

Follow the keyboard focus

Figure 3-10

Pointer size

Pointer color

Figure 3-11

7. The Other Options settings control various and sundry items:

- Play Animations in Windows controls whether Windows apps start and close with an animation sequence. If you prefer not to see animation sequences when an app is launched or closed, turn this switch to the off position.

- Show Windows Background controls whether images can appear on the Start screen. If this switch is off, images don't appear on the screen and you can't choose an image in the Personalize panel. (See the next section in this chapter, "Change the Start Screen Background," for more information.)

- Show Notifications For controls how long certain pop-up messages appear before disappearing. These notifications are sometimes called *tooltips* or *toasts* (because of the way they pop up). By default, notifications disappear after 5 seconds, which usually isn't enough time to read a long notification. Note that notifications disappear when you move the mouse or select another option. I suggest that you try 30 seconds for the delay.

- Cursor Thickness, the last setting, controls the width of the vertical blinking line that appears when you can type text. The box on the left under this heading displays the current cursor (without blinking). To try a different thickness, drag the selection box to the right. (You might try a cursor thickness of 2 or 3 pixels.)

 More Ease of Access settings are available through the desktop. The settings are easiest to access by pressing ■+U (for *usability*). In the Ease of Access Center, as shown in **Figure 3-12**, you can choose many access settings.

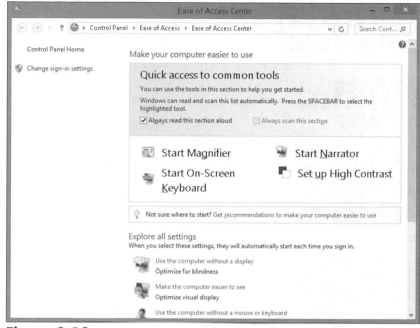

Figure 3-12

Change the Start Screen Background

1. On the Start screen, display the charms bar (refer to **Figure 3-1**) and select Settings with one of these methods:

- **Mouse:** Move the mouse pointer into the lower-right corner of the screen to display the charms bar, and then click Settings.

- **Touchscreen:** Swipe from the right edge of the screen to display the charms bar, and then tap Settings.

- **Keyboard:** Press ■+I to go straight to Settings, skipping the charms bar.

2. The Settings panel appears (refer to **Figure 3-2**). Select Personalize. The Personalize panel opens, as shown in **Figure 3-13**.

Figure 3-13

You see the Start screen more often than any other screen, so personalize it to make it yours.

3. Using a click or a tap, select one of the 20 images. You immediately see your choice on the Start screen.

If you'd like a solid color background, with no image behind the tiles on the Start screen, select the blank image.

4. Using a click or a tap, select a background color. Try different colors until you find one that suits you.

5. Using a click or tap, select an accent color. Again, experiment with the accent colors until you find a suitable one.

6. Click the Start screen to apply your background choices and close the Personalize panel.

Working with User Accounts

*W*indows 8.1 seeks out an Internet connection automatically from the moment you start it. More often than not, you connect to the Internet using a wireless or *Wi-Fi* connection. For this reason, if you start a laptop or tablet in a coffee shop or library, you may see a notification that one or more network connections are available. That's convenient.

A computer without an Internet connection is an island, if not a paperweight. Connecting to a network, however, opens a door to your computer — and malefactors try to push through that door to access your computer. Windows 8.1 has a *firewall* that monitors and restricts traffic in and out. Don't be afraid of connecting to the Internet, but be aware of the risks and be careful to which networks you connect. In Chapter 1, you create a local user account. You need a Microsoft account to take full advantage of Windows 8.1 features such as the Microsoft Store for apps (see Chapter 9), SkyDrive for online storage, and synchronizing settings between computers. In this chapter, you create a Microsoft account and choose a secure method for logging into your account. You also discover how to switch from a local account to a Microsoft account.

To control access to your computer, you find out how to use a password, a shorter personal identification number (*PIN*), or even a personal photo to unlock your computer.

 If other people use your computer, you may want to create more than one user account. If each person who uses the computer has a separate account, you can keep data, apps, and settings tidy and private.

Even if you're the only one using your computer, you may want more than one account. For example, if you create a new local user account, you can experiment with the new account — changing the look and function of Windows 8.1 — without affecting your first account.

 Many of the steps in this chapter involve entering text, such as your name. If you don't have a physical keyboard, use the virtual keyboard, which is covered in Chapter 1.

Connect to the Internet

1. On the Start screen, display the charms bar (shown in **Figure** 4-1) using one of these methods:

- **Mouse:** Place the mouse pointer in the lower-right corner of the screen and move the pointer up.

- **Touchscreen:** Drag your finger from the right edge of the screen to the left.

- **Keyboard:** Press ⊞+C.

2. To the left of the time and date is a network connection icon. Refer to Table 4-1 to determine which network connection icon appears on your screen.

Network indicator

Charms bar

Figure 4-1

Table 4-1	Network Connection Icons
Icon	***What It Means***
	You aren't connected but wireless (Wi-Fi) connections are available. The more solid bars, the stronger the connection.
	A wireless connection has been established.
	A wired connection has been established. Your computer is plugged into a router, a device that connects to the phone company's DSL or to cable TV.
	You have no current connection and no available connections. (The x can appear over a plug, as it does here, or over bars.)

3. Select the Settings charm. In the Settings panel on the right, you see the network connection icon again. The Network icon indicates information about the current network connection, if any (refer to Table 4-1). The icon itself will indicate whether the connection is wired (a plug) or wireless (five bars). Under the icon, you may see one of the following:

  - **Network name:** If you are connected to a wired or wireless network, the name of the network will appear below the icon. In that case, you're all set, but keep reading.

  - *Available*: A wireless connection that you may be able to connect to is available.

  - *Unavailable*: No connection has been established or is available.

 Select or choose options by moving the mouse pointer and left-clicking or by tapping a touchscreen with your finger.

4. Select the Network icon. The Networks panel appears, as shown in **Figure 4-2,** and lists all available network connections. There may be no connections or dozens.

 If you see *Not connected* and *No connections available*, you may be out of luck. Check your computer documentation to see whether your PC has wireless capability and whether you need to turn on a mechanical switch. The Troubleshoot button on the screen opens Help on the desktop. See Chapter 5 for information on using the desktop.

 If your computer is near a router (DSL or cable) and you don't have wireless capability, connect your PC and the router using an Ethernet cable, which is thicker than a phone line, with wider connections. Ethernet cables may be yellow or green.

Available wireless connections

Figure 4-2

5. Select a connection. Note that not all displayed connections are accessible or desirable.

 If you're not sure you can trust a connection, you might want to forego a connection — better safe than sorry. (Unsafe wireless connections can be used to eavesdrop on your activities, though that scenario is rare.) However, if an available connection sports the name of the establishment you're in or near, such as a restaurant or a coffee shop, the connection may be safe. The same is true of connections at libraries, airports, and many other public spaces.

 Generally, you want to select the connection with the strongest signal (most white bars). In addition, consider the connection speed. Hover the mouse pointer over a network tile, and you may see Type: 802.11, which is the general standard for wireless (Wi-Fi) connections. A letter at the end of that number indicates a slower connection (g) or faster one (n). If two connections are otherwise identical, (n) is preferable.

6. After you select a connection, the selected tile expands and displays the Connect Automatically check box, as shown in **Figure 4-3.** If you trust the connection and might want to use it again, leave the check box selected. Otherwise, deselect the check box. To continue, select the Connect button.

Connect automatically the next time

Figure 4-3

7. You may be prompted to enter a network security key (a series of characters), which limits access to those who know the key. See **Figure 4-4.** The key protects that network and its users. If you're using a hotel's connection, you can obtain the key from the front desk. If you don't know the key, select Cancel. Otherwise, enter the key (dots appear as you type) and select Next.

 If the connection is public and open, you won't be prompted for a key. Open connections are common in libraries, coffee shops, and other places many people come and go.

A secure network requires a key

Figure 4-4

 If you have access to your *router*, which is a kind of network device connected to the phone line or cable TV, the router may have a button you can push to connect without using the security key.

8. If you entered the correct key or none was required, you may see this message: *Do you want to turn on sharing between PCs and connect to devices on this network? Sharing* refers to allowing computers access to your files or to a device, such as a printer. You should share at home but not in a public location. Choose one of the following:

- **No:** This option prevents you from connecting directly with other computers and protects your computer from networks in public places. You'll still have Internet access.

- **Yes:** This option enables you to share documents and devices between your computers on a home or office network.

 If you're not sure about which option to choose, go with No.

9. When a Wi-Fi connection is established, *Connected* appears next to the network name in the Networks panel (**Figure** 4-5, left). The connection name and signal strength appear in the Settings panel (**Figure** 4-5, middle). Now display the charms bar (see Step 1 for help). The connection strength (but not the name) appears next to the time and date (**Figure** 4-5, right).

Figure 4-5

 If you selected the Connect Automatically check box (in Step 6), the connection will be used anytime it is available. If you move your computer to another location out of range of this network (usually a few hundred yards), you will have to repeat these steps to connect to another network.

10. To turn off or disconnect the network connection, display the Networks panel again (Steps 1–4). Select the connected network (see **Figure 4-6**) and then select the Disconnect button. (If you disconnect this network, reconnect before continuing.)

 Most of the time, you'll stay connected. When you shut down the computer or move the computer far enough away from the connection, it disconnects automatically.

Select to disconnect

Figure 4-6

Create a New Microsoft Account

1. Follow these steps to switch your Windows 8.1 user account from a local account to a Microsoft account and in so doing create a Microsoft account. On the Start screen, select your name in the upper-right corner of the screen. In the pop-up menu that appears (see **Figure** 4-7), choose Change Account Picture. The Accounts screen appears. Your account information appears with *Local Account* under your name, as shown in **Figure** 4-8.

Select for fast access to the
Accounts screen

Figure 4-7

If you see don't see *Local Account*, you already have a Microsoft account and don't need to follow these steps.

(←) Accounts   ⌕

Your account

Sign-in options

Other accounts

Peter W
Local Account

Sign in with a Microsoft account to easily get your online email, photos, files and settings (like browser history and favorites) on all your devices.

Connect to a Microsoft account

Figure 4-8

2. Select the Connect to a Microsoft Account link. Enter your current password (if any) and select Next. The Sign in to Your Microsoft Account screen appears. To create a new account, select the Create a New Account link (at the bottom of the screen).

3. On the Create a Microsoft Account screen (see **Figure 4-9**), in the Email Address box, type the name you want to use (no spaces). Common names have probably been claimed by others and are unavailable. If you type a name that is already taken, you'll get an error message to that effect, but not until several steps later (you can change your choice then). Unusual names, especially full names, may work. Adding some numbers to your name may make it unique, such as *your-firstname-lastname*-12345.

4. Next to the @ sign after your name, choose between one of the available services. I know of no specific advantage to one or the other service.

Enter your information

Figure 4-9

5. In the New Password box, type a password. Dots appear instead of what you type. Use at least 8 characters. Mix uppercase and lowercase, numbers, and symbols such as hyphens (but no spaces).

> Your password should be easy enough for you to remember and type, but not easy for someone else to guess. Don't use the names of any family members (including pets). A good password can be difficult to create, so try this trick: Think of a memorable phrase or lyric. Next, use the first letter from each word, capitalizing some of those letters. Then substitute some letters with numbers (for example, 3 for the letter *E* or the number 0 for the letter *O*). Don't put your password on a sticky note near your screen.

6. In the Re-Enter Password box, type the same password. If this password doesn't match the one in Step 5, the message *These passwords don't match* appears next to the box.

7. Type your first and last names in the appropriate boxes.

8. If your country or region is not preselected, select your country. Use any of the following methods to move through the list to your country name:

- **Mouse:** Click in the box. Roll the mouse wheel up or down. Click your country name.

- **Touchscreen:** Drag the list up or down. Tap your country name.

- **Keyboard:** Type the first letter of your country or use the arrow keys to move up and down the list. With your country selected, press the Enter or Tab key.

9. Review your entries. Select the Next button. The Add Security Info screen appears, as shown in **Figure 14-10**.

10. Select the month, day, and year of your birth. (You can lie, if you remember your response.)

11. In the Phone box, select your country again (using the methods in Step 8). In the next box, enter your phone number, including area code. If you have to reset your password, Microsoft may use this number to confirm your identity.

12. If you have an alternate e-mail address, you can type it in the Alternate Email box. The alternate e-mail address enables you to receive e-mail from Microsoft if you can't access the account you're setting up.

Figure 4-10

13. In the box next to Secret Question, select one.

14. In the Answer box, type an answer to the selected question. Hint: The answer doesn't have to be true, just memorable and at least 5 characters. Your answer to the selected question may be used to verify your identity. Because case and punctuation matter, remember your answer exactly as you type it. Then select Next.

15. On the Communications Preferences screen, shown in **Figure 4-11**, select the first check box if you want to allow Microsoft to monitor your online activity so that it can target online advertisements to your screen based on your user profile and history of surfing the web.

Figure 4-11

16. If you don't want to receive promotional offers and surveys, select the check box to remove the check mark from the second check box.

17. In the Enter These Characters box, you see some odd characters. This test eliminates non-humans from creating an account (seriously). In the box below those characters, type what you see.

 If you can't recognize the characters, select New for a different set of characters or Audio to have the characters read aloud.

18. You can select the links to the Microsoft services agreement and privacy and cookies statement if you want to read what you're about to agree with. Be the first.

19. Select the Next button. The Help Us Protect Your Info screen appears. Choose an option for being informed in the event that Microsoft detects what it thinks is someone misusing your account. Choose to be informed by a text message, telephone call, or e-mail message. (You can select the I Can't Do This Right Now link if you want.) Then click Next.

20. In the Enter the Code You Received screen, enter the code Microsoft sent to you. Then click Next.

21. Click Next in the screen that tells you some of the bene-fits of having a Microsoft account.

22. On the Switch to a Microsoft Account screen, select the Switch button to start using your Microsoft account.

 Skip the section "Use an Existing E-Mail Address for a Microsoft Account."

Switch from a Local to an Existing Microsoft Account

1. Follow these steps to switch your Windows 8.1 user account from a local account to your existing Microsoft account. On the Start screen, select your name in the upper-right corner of the screen, and then choose Change Account Picture from the pop-up menu that appears (refer to **Figure** 4-7). The Accounts screen opens. Your account information appears with *Local Account* under your name. Refer to **Figure** 4-8.

 If you don't have a Microsoft account already, see "Create a New E-Mail Address for a Microsoft Account."

 If you don't see *Local Account* under your user account name, you're already signed in with your Microsoft.

2. Select the Connect to a Microsoft Account link. On the Switch to a Microsoft Account screen, enter the password to your local account (if any) and select Next. The screen shown in **Figure** 4-12 appears. Type the e-mail address of your Microsoft Account as well as the password. Then select the Next button.

3. Confirm the Security verification data. When you set up your Microsoft account, you chose how to receive the code you need to activate your Microsoft account. Select Next.

4. The Enter the Code You Received screen appears. Open your e-mail service and obtain the code. It arrives in an e-mail from the Microsoft Account Team. Enter the code and choose Next until you come to the Switch to a Microsoft Account on This PC screen. Select the Switch button. Note your account name and associated e-mail address on the Accounts screen.

⊕ Sign in to your Microsoft account

Sign in to easily get your online email, photos, files, and settings (like browser history and favorites) on all your devices. You can manage your synced settings at any time.

Don't have an account?

Next   Cancel

Figure 4-12

Add a User Account

1. You already have the only user account you require on your computer. However, you may want to create an account for someone in your household or as a practice account. Select your name on the Start screen. Choose Change Account Picture from the menu that appears (refer to **Figure** 4-7). The Accounts screen appears.

2. On the left, select Other Accounts. On the right, select Add an Account. The How Will This Person Sign In screen appears.

 If you can't select Add an Account, return to the Start screen. Select your name and choose Sign Out. On the Sign In screen, choose the account you created in Chapter 1.

3. At the bottom of the How Will This Person Sign In screen, choose Sign in without a Microsoft Account to create a local account.

 If you know you want a Microsoft Account instead of a local account, jump to "Create a New Microsoft Account" or "Switch from a Local to an Existing Microsoft Account" earlier in this chapter.

4. On the next screen, read the explanation of your two options for signing in. Then select the Local Account button.

5. On the next screen (see **Figure** 4-13), enter the user name in the first box. Use the person's first name, last name, first and last name, initials, nickname — something easy to remember and type.

Only the user name is required for a local account

Figure 4-13

 You are not required to use a password with a local account, which makes signing in easy. However, without a password, anyone can use the computer and access information you might want to protect.

6. In the Password box, enter a password. Dots will appear for each character you type.

 For suggestions on creating a good password, see the tip in Step 5 in the section, "Create a New Microsoft Account," earlier in this chapter.

7. In the Reenter Password box, type the same password exactly.

8. In the Password Hint box, type a reminder only you will understand.

For laptops or other portable devices, consider using your phone number with area code as the hint (if you're sure you don't need a real hint). The hint appears when someone tries and fails to enter log-in information. By including your phone number, you might help an honest person return your lost, stolen, or misplaced device to you.

9. After completing all the available boxes, choose the Next button. You may see an error message if you left a required field empty, your passwords don't match, or the user name already exists on this computer. If you do see an error, correct your mistake and choose Next again.

10. On the final screen, shown in **Figure 4-14,** you see the new user name next to a generic user picture. Note the option to indicate that this new account belongs to a child. Select this option if you want to receive e-mail reports on the child's computer usage. Select the Finish button. The Accounts screen appears, with the new user name under Other Accounts.

 If family safety options interest you, type **family** on the Start screen, select Settings on the right, and then select Family Safety on the left. The Family Safety function opens on the desktop.

11. Return to the Start screen. In the upper-right corner of the screen, select your user name. In the drop-down menu that appears, select the new user name to switch to that account.

12. A screen appears with the new user name. If you used a password on the new user account, type that password in the box and select the on-screen right arrow or press Enter.

The new user name

Figure 4-14

 The first time you sign in as a new user, you have to wait a moment while apps are installed for the new user. Soon the generic Start screen appears. (Any settings you changed in your account do not transfer to other accounts.)

13. In the upper-right corner of the Start screen, choose the new user name. Note that the old user name is labeled *Signed In*, as shown in **Figure 4-15**. Both accounts are signed in. You can switch between them by selecting the user name you want to switch to. To sign out of an account, choose Sign Out.

All users are listed here

Figure 4-15

 For information on personalizing the Lock and Start screens for the new account, see Chapter 3.

Create a Password

1. On the Start screen, select your name. From the drop-down menu that appears, choose Change Account Picture (refer to **Figure 4-7**). The Accounts screen appears.

 If you already have a password, see the section "Change or Remove Your Password."

2. On the left, select Sign-in Options.

3. If you don't have a password but want one, select the Add button under Passwords.

 The buttons available under Sign-in Options depend on your current setup. You may see buttons that enable you to create, change, or remove a particular setting.

4. In the Create a Password screen, shown in **Figure** 4-16, enter a password in the New Password box.

Create a password

New password

Reenter password

Password hint

Next   Cancel

Figure 4-16

 For a local account, the password can be any length. See Step 5 in the section, "Create a New Microsoft Account," for suggestions about creating a good password

5. In the Reenter Password box, enter the password again.

6. Enter a hint to remind yourself — and no one else — about your password.

7. Select Next. If any error messages appear, correct the entries and select Next again.

8. The final Create a Password screen indicates you must use your new password the next time you sign in. Select Finish.

Change or Remove Your Password

1. On the Start screen, select your name, and then choose Change Account Picture. On the left side of the Accounts screen, select Sign-in Options.

2. If you want to change your password, select the Change button.

 If you don't have a password but want one, see the section "Create a Password."

3. On the Change Your Password screen, enter your current password and then select the Next button.

4. On the next Change Your Password screen (see **Figure 4-17**), enter the new password.

 To remove your current password and use no password, leave all boxes blank.

For a local account, the password can be any length. Microsoft account passwords must be between 7 and 16 characters and sufficiently complex, as determined by Windows 8.1.

5. In the Reenter Password box, enter the password again.

6. Enter a hint to remind yourself — and no one else — about your password. Then select Next. If any error messages appear, correct the entries and select Next again.

7. The final screen indicates you must use your new password the next time you sign in. (This message appears even if you left the password blank, in which case you won't need any password.) Select Finish.

If you don't want a password, leave these boxes blank

Figure 4-17

Create a PIN

1. A *PIN* (personal identification number) has two advantages over a password. One, a PIN consists of just four numbers, so it's easier to remember and enter, especially with a virtual keyboard. Two, you don't press the Enter key with a PIN, making it even faster to use. (I use a PIN on my home computer.) On the Start screen, select your user name and then choose Change Account Picture.

2. On the Accounts screen, select Sign-in Options. Select the Add button under PIN.

If you have a PIN but want to change or remove it, see the section "Change or Remove Your Pin."

 You can't create a picture password or PIN if you don't have a regular password. See the section "Create a Password."

3. On the next screen, enter your current password and then select OK.

4. On the Create a PIN screen, shown in **Figure** 4-18, enter four digits in the first box. Re-enter those four digits in the second box. Select Finish. The next time you sign in, enter your four-digit pin.

Create a PIN

A PIN is a quick, convenient way to sign in to this PC by using a 4-digit code.

Enter PIN

Confirm PIN

Finish   Cancel

Figure 4-18

 On the sign-in screen, you can switch to a password screen, even if you have a PIN. This feature enables you to sign in if you don't remember your PIN.

Change or Remove Your PIN

1. Select your name on the Start screen, and then choose Change Account Picture. On the Accounts screen, select Sign-in Options.

2. If you don't want to use a PIN, select the Remove button under PIN. One click and the PIN is gone without further confirmation. Skip the remaining steps.

 If you don't have a PIN but want one, see the section "Create a PIN."

3. If you want to change your PIN, select the Change button. On the verification screen, enter your current password and select OK.

4. On the Change Your PIN screen, enter a new four-digit PIN in the first box.

5. In the Confirm New PIN box, reenter your new PIN. (A message appears if the PINs don't match.) Select Finish. The next time you sign in, enter your new four-digit pin.

Delete a User Account

1. Before you delete a user account, make sure that account is signed out. Then sign in to the administrator account, which is the one you created in Chapter 1.

2. Select your name on the Start screen, and then choose Change Account Picture. On the Accounts screen, select Other Accounts to open the Other Accounts screen (see **Figure 4-19**).

Select a user to delete

Other accounts

Add a user

Bobby
Local Account

Edit   Remove

Figure 4-19

3. Select the account you want to delete. Then select the Remove button.

4. In the Delete Account and Data window, select the Delete Account and Data button.

 Take heed of the onscreen warning. Deleting a user account removes the user's data, including all documents, music, and other files. If you're not sure which option is best, choose Keep Files or Cancel.

5. Return to the Start screen by clicking in the lower-left corner of the screen, by swiping from the right edge to the left and tapping Start, or by pressing ⊞.

Getting Comfortable with the Desktop

*I*n Windows 8.1, the *desktop* is an app you access through a tile on the Start screen. Unlike other apps, the desktop is an environment for using programs that pre-date the new Windows 8.1 apps. The desktop enables Windows 8.1 users to run older programs. Microsoft takes pains not to break abruptly with the past as it paves the way for the future.

You may find yourself on the desktop as a result of choosing an app from the Start screen, Search Results screen, or All Apps screen. For that reason alone, take the time to explore the desktop-way of doing things, which is not quite the new Windows 8.1 way.

One key feature of the desktop is the *taskbar*, a strip along the bottom of the screen that shows icons for desktop programs. The taskbar can be used to run and switch between desktop programs. Most programs on the desktop run in windows, as opposed to the full-screen nature of Windows 8.1 apps.

In this chapter, you get acquainted with the desktop, the taskbar, and windowed apps. You change the date, time, and time zone, as needed. You resize and reposition windowed apps. You select a background for the desktop and make some desktop apps more convenient to use by pinning them to the taskbar. Finally, you work with the Task Manager, which lets you end any app — desktop or Windows 8.1.

 The desktop originated when using the mouse was the most common method for selecting objects (touchscreens were nonexistent). Therefore, on the desktop, a few tasks are easier to do with the mouse than with touch or keyboard.

 This chapter is an introduction to the desktop. See Part IV to dive a little deeper into desktop functions, such as organizing documents.

Check Out the Desktop

1. On the Start screen, select the Desktop tile to display the desktop. Your desktop will have a picture in the background.

 Another way to display the desktop when you are looking at the Start screen is to press ■+Tab.

2. Examine your desktop for *icons* — small pictures that represent either programs, which perform functions, or documents, such as letters and photos. You select an icon to run a program or open a document. The Windows 8.1 desktop displays an icon for the Recycle Bin, where deleted documents go. The Recycle Bin may be the only icon on your desktop, or you may see others. See Chapter 14 for information on using the Recycle Bin.

3. The area at the bottom of the screen is the *taskbar*, where you see icons for some programs as shown in **Figure 5-1**. The first two icons, for example, are for programs that are available but not currently running (Microsoft Internet Explorer and File Explorer, respectively).

Taskbar Icon tray

Figure 5-1

 You can use the taskbar to switch between programs by selecting the icon for the program you want to use.

 Yet another way to get from the Start screen to the desktop is to click the Start button. Hover the pointer over the lower-left corner of the screen. When the Start button appears, select it.

4. The right end of the taskbar is an area called the *icon tray,* which displays the icons for other programs that run automatically when your computer starts. Select an icon in the icon tray to open the associated program. The date and time are to the right of the icon tray.

 You select items on the desktop or in the taskbar by clicking with the mouse or tapping the touchscreen. To some extent, you can use the Tab and arrow keys, but that's an awkward method.

 If you have a touchscreen, note the taskbar icon for the virtual keyboard. See Chapter 1 for information about using the keyboard.

5. Right-click over an icon or tap and hold until a small box appears, then release. A *context menu* appears with options specific to the icon you selected. Select anywhere else on the desktop to dismiss this menu. Repeat this on a few different areas of the screen to see how the context menu changes.

 If you can select the item using the keyboard, you can then press the context menu key to display the menu.

Change the Date or Time

1. Select the date and time displayed in the taskbar. A calendar and clock pop up, as shown in **Figure 5-2**.

Figure 5-2

2. If the date or time is incorrect, select Change Date and Time Settings. In the Date and Time window that appears, select the Change Date and Time button.

3. In the Date and Time Settings window, shown in **Figure 5-3**, select the correct date in the calendar. Then change the time by using the little triangles that point up (later) or down (earlier) or by entering the specific hours and minutes. Select OK to keep your change or Cancel to ignore your change.

4. Back in the Date and Time window, select Change Time Zone.

5. In the Time Zone Settings window, shown in **Figure 5-4**, select the Time Zone drop-down menu and then select your time zone. Select (add a check mark) or deselect the Daylight Saving Time option as appropriate. Select OK to keep your change or Cancel to ignore your change.

1. Select the date

2. Change the time

Figure 5-3

Select your time zone

Figure 5-4

Explore the Parts of a Window

1. In the taskbar, select the second icon from the left, which looks like a folder. File Explorer opens, as shown in **Figure 5-5**.

Quick Access toolbar

File Explorer icon   File Explorer window

Figure 5-5

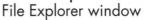 File Explorer enables you to view your computer storage, such as hard disks, and folders, which are used to organize your documents. See Chapter 14 for information on using File Explorer.

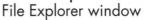 File Explorer is not the same as Microsoft Internet Explorer, the web browser (and the first icon in the taskbar). See Chapter 6 for information on using Microsoft Internet Explorer to browse the Web.

2. Explore the example window in **Figure** 5-5, starting at the top left:

- **Quick Access toolbar:** The *Quick Access toolbar* gives you fast access to common operations, such as saving a document. This toolbar is not present in all windows and may feature different functions, depending on the window.

- **Title bar:** The *title bar, which* is the top line of the window, contains the title of the desktop program you're using. When you use a program to create a document, the name of the document also appears in the title bar.

The title of the window in **Figure 5-5** is This PC, the location File Explorer is focused on when you open File Explorer.

- *Minimize:* The *Minimize button* shrinks or hides the window's contents. The program that the window contains is still running and open, but the window is out of sight. You'll still see the program's icon in the taskbar. Select the Minimize button when you want to ignore a particular window but aren't actually done with it. To restore the window, select its icon in the taskbar.

- *Maximize/Restore:* The *Maximize button* (the button with a single square) fills the screen with the contents of the window. Select the Maximize button to hide the desktop and other open windows, to concentrate on one window, and to see as much of the window's contents as you can. The *Restore button* (the button with two squares) is the name of the button that appears after you select the Maximize button; it replaces the Maximize button. Select the Restore button to return the window to its previous size, which is between maximized and minimized. (Press ■+up arrow key to maximize, and ■+down arrow key to restore or minimize.)

- *Close: The Close button* is the red button with the X in the top-right corner of the window. Select the Close button when you are done with the window. Close is also called Quit and Exit. (Press Alt+F4 to close the current window or the desktop itself. This keyboard shortcut works for Windows 8.1 apps, as well.)

- **Ribbon:** The *ribbon* is a toolbar that provides access to many functions organized as groups within tabs. The tabs appear across the top of the ribbon. The first time you run File Explorer, the ribbon is hidden (collapsed). Display the ribbon by selecting the caret symbol (^) on the far right, next to Help (the question mark). Select the caret again to hide the ribbon. You can also press Ctrl+F1 to toggle the ribbon on and off. (Leave the ribbon visible for this chapter.) The tabs remain in view and function the same. Although ribbons vary between programs, most ribbons have File and View tabs. To use a tab, select its name to display its functions, and then select the item you want to use.

 The ribbon can help you discover new functions.

- **Contents:** The bulk of the window contains the program or document you're using. File Explorer displays locations on the left and objects in that location on the right.

- **Status bar:** Along the bottom edge of the window, some programs display information about the window or its contents in a single-line *status bar*. File Explorer does not have a status bar.

 Scan the edges of windows. Often, important information and functions are pushed to these edges around the main content area.

3. Select the Close button (the red X) to close File Explorer.

 Although the Quick Access toolbar and the Close button work on a touchscreen, they are small targets. You may find a stylus more accurate when dealing with smaller elements.

 See Chapter 2 for information on finding other desktop programs, such as the Calculator.

Resize a Window

1. To resize a window, open File Explorer by selecting the folder icon in the taskbar. (Refer to **Figure 5-5**.)

 2. If the window is maximized (fills the screen), select the Restore button to make the window smaller.

3. Use one of these methods to resize the window:

- **Mouse:** Move the mouse pointer to the right edge of the window, until the pointer changes to a double-headed arrow called the *resize pointer*. Click and drag the edge of the window, using the resize pointer. (To drag, click and hold down the mouse button while you move the mouse.)

- **Touchscreen:** Drag the right edge of the window.

 Drag left to shrink the window and right to expand it.

4. Resize the window's width and height at the same time by dragging a corner of the window (see **Figure 5-6**). If you want a challenge, try resizing the top-right corner without accidentally selecting the Close button.

Drag the corner with the mouse or your finger to resize the window
Figure 5-6

5. Resize the window's width *or* height by dragging any of
   the four sides.

> You may want to resize a window to show only what
> you need to see, nothing more. Practice resizing from
> any side or corner.

6. Leave the window open as you go on to the next task.

Arrange Some Windows

1. On the desktop, select and open the Recycle Bin by double-clicking or double-tapping its icon. The Recycle Bin
   contains deleted files and folders. It appears in another
   File Explorer window. See **Figure 5-7**.

Double-click by clicking the left mouse button twice, without a pause. Double-tap by tapping twice in quick succession.

2. If File Explorer isn't still open from the preceding section, open it by selecting the folder icon in the taskbar. You now see two overlapping windows on the desktop (refer to **Figure** 5-7), one titled *This PC* and the other titled *Recycle Bin*.

 The window in front of the others is called the *active* window. All other windows are *inactive*. Note that the title bar of the active window is a different color from the title bar in any inactive window. Selecting anywhere in an inactive window makes it active and moves it to the front of the others.

Figure 5-7

3. Drag the Recycle Bin title bar (avoiding the buttons on the left and right ends) to move that window a little.

4. Drag the This PC title bar (again, avoiding the buttons on both ends). The This PC window moves in front of the Recycle Bin as you move it. Move both windows so that you can see a little of each, as in **Figure 5-8**.

5. Practice moving both windows. Arranging windows helps you see and do more than one thing at a time. Use the techniques from the section "Resize a Window" to see as much as you can of both windows at once.

 If you can't see the title bar of the window you want to move, move the other window to uncover the hidden title bar.

Move a window by dragging its title bar

Figure 5-8

6. Leave both windows open for the following task.

Snap a Window

1. Drag one of the windows you worked with in the preceding section to the left edge of the screen. When the mouse pointer or your finger touches the left edge of the screen, you'll see an outline on the screen, as shown in **Figure 5-9**. Release the window, and it resizes automatically to fill the left half of the screen, as shown in **Figure 5-10**. This procedure is called *snap*. (To snap a window using the keyboard, press ⊞+left arrow.)

Drag the window to the far left   Note the outline

Figure 5-9

Release the window to complete the snap

Figure 5-10

2. Now snap the other window to the right. (To move the window using the keyboard, press ⊞+right arrow.) It resizes and fills the right half of the screen.

 When two or more windows are displayed side by side like this, they are called **tiled** windows.

3. Drag either window by the title bar away from the edge of the screen. The window returns to its previous size.

4. Drag either window to the top edge of the screen. This action maximizes the window, just as though you selected the Maximize button (see the section "Explore the Parts of a Window").

5. Drag the title bar of the maximized window away from the top to restore it to its previous size, just as though you selected the Restore button.

6. Close or minimize both windows.

Choose a Desktop Background

1. On the desktop, display the Settings panel, shown in **Figure 5-11,** using one of these methods:

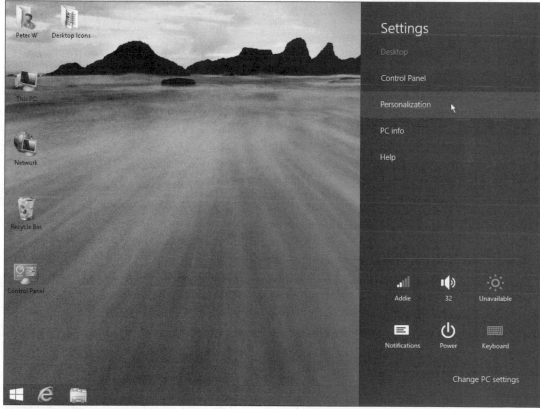

Figure 5-11

- **Mouse:** Move the mouse pointer to the top-right or bottom-right corner to display the charms bar. Click the Settings charm.

- **Touchscreen:** Swipe from the right edge to display the charms bar. Tap the Settings charm.

- **Keyboard:** Press ⊞+I.

2. Select Personalization. The Personalization window opens, as shown in **Figure 5-12**.

Select Desktop Background

Figure 5-12

You can use the Personalization window to customize many aspects of the desktop. The more time you spend on the desktop and not on the Start screen, the more worthwhile this personalization may be.

3. In the Personalization window, select the Desktop Background option (at the bottom). The Desktop Background window appears, as shown in **Figure 5-13**.

4. Select any photo to make that photo the desktop background. The background changes immediately. To see the entire desktop, minimize the current window. Restore the Desktop Background window by selecting its icon in the taskbar or by repeating the preceding steps.

 The background you choose here will also appear on the Desktop tile on the Start screen. That's pretty cool.

Select a photo

Figure 5-13

5. Select more than one photo for the background as
follows:

- Select individual photos using the check box in the
  upper-left corner of each thumbnail. Select again
  to remove that check mark.

- Select all photos under a heading, such as Earth,
  by selecting the heading.

- Use the Select All button to select all photos.
  (Yeah, that was obvious.) Select the Clear All button to unselect all photos.

6. Select the Change Picture Every option to change the
amount of time that passes before the next picture is displayed. Intervals range from every 10 seconds to once per
day. For a quick test of this feature, choose 10 seconds.

7. If you want to mix the order in which the photos appear,
select the Shuffle check box.

8. Minimize the Desktop Background window. The desktop
background changes every 10 seconds (unless you chose
a different frequency or chose only one photo). Restore
the Desktop Background window by selecting its icon on
the taskbar.

 Open the Picture Location drop-down menu and
choose Pictures Library, Top Rated Photos (based on
ratings you give to your own photos), or Solid Colors
(such as white) to access other ways to choose a
desktop background. See Chapter 10 for information
on adding photos to the Pictures Library.

9. To keep the selections you make in the Desktop
Background window, select the Save Changes button
(refer to **Figure 5-13**). To undo those selections, select
Cancel. In either case, you return to the Personalization

window. Close the Personalization window when you are done with it.

Pin Icons to the Taskbar

1. On the Start screen, select the All Apps button to display the Apps screen. The All Apps button is the downward-pointing arrow in the lower-left corner of the Start screen.

2. In the Search box, type *calculator* to search for that desktop program. Then select the Calculator tile and display the app bar, shown in **Figure 5-14**, using one of these methods:

Select this button to pin a desktop application to the taskbar
Figure 5-14

- **Mouse:** Right-click the Calculator tile.

- **Touchscreen:** Swipe the Calculator tile down or up slightly.

 - **Keyboard:** Press the Tab key to highlight the Calculator tile. Press the context menu key, usually found to the right of the spacebar.

3. Select the Pin to Taskbar button. Doing so places the icon for Calculator in the desktop taskbar for easy access.

4. Switch to the Start screen. Then display the desktop by selecting the Desktop tile on the Start screen.

 Keyboard: Press ⊞+D to go directly to the desktop.

5. The Calculator icon appears in the taskbar, as shown in **Figure 5-15**.

Calculator is pinned

Figure 5-15

6. Return to the Start screen. Repeat Steps 1 and 2 and then select Unpin from Taskbar.

7. Switch to the desktop. The Calculator icon is gone.

 You can pin desktop apps to the Start screen in addition to or instead of the desktop. Windows 8.1 apps can be pinned only to the Start screen.

Pinned icons have a killer feature: *jumplists*, which are short menus of tasks and documents specific to the pinned app. To see the jumplist of a pinned app, right-click its icon in the taskbar or tap and hold on the icon until a small box appears. Try that with the File Explorer icon in the taskbar. Not all desktop apps have jumplists.

Stop Apps with the Task Manager

1. On the desktop, select Task Manager from the taskbar context menu (shown in **Figure 5-16**) using one of these methods:

- **Mouse:** Right-click over an empty area of the taskbar and select Task Manager from the context menu.

- **Touchscreen:** Tap and hold an empty area of the taskbar until a small box appears, then release. Select Task Manager from the context menu.

- **Keyboard:** Press Ctrl+Shift+Esc to display the Task Manager directly.

 You can search for Task Manager from the Start screen. Then, you could pin it to Start or the taskbar.

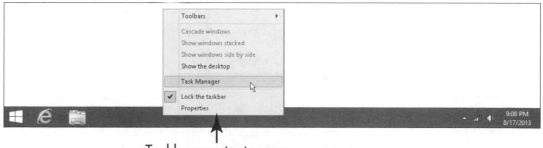

Taskbar context menu

Figure 5-16

2. The Task Manager lists any running apps — both desktop apps, such as Calculator, and Windows 8.1 apps, such as Weather. Select an app, also referred to as a *task*. Note that the End Task button is now available, as shown in **Figure 5-17**. You don't have to end this task, but you could. Any of the tasks in the Task Manager window can be ended without consequences.

> Be careful about ending an app used to create something (for example, a word-processing app) because you could lose data you haven't saved before ending the task. Use the Task Manager to end tasks that you can't end otherwise, such as a frozen or locked app or one that seems to slow down everything.

Select a task

Figure 5-17

3. Select the More Details option. The Task Manager expands and displays detailed information about every process running on the computer. There's more to Task Manager, although you may not need all of its capabilities. Select Fewer Details to return to the simpler version.

4. Close the Task Manager, and then return to the Start screen.

Part II
Windows 8.1 and the Web

Visit www.dummies.com/extras/windows8dot1forseniors for instructions for adding a program tile to the Start screen.

Finding What You Need on the Web

Chapter 6

*T*he World Wide Web — or, simply, the Web — provides quick access to information and entertainment worldwide. One part library, one part marketplace, and one part soapbox, the Web makes everything equidistant: From down the block to halfway around the world — even out into space — everything is a few clicks or taps away. News, shopping, and the electronic equivalent of the town square await you.

You explore the Web using a *web browser*, a program designed to make browsing the Web easy, enjoyable, and safe. In this chapter, I show how you can use Microsoft Internet Explorer to step beyond your computer into the global village.

You browse *web pages*, which are published by governments, businesses, and individuals — anyone can create web pages. Each web page may consist of a few words or thousands of words and pictures. A web page is part of a larger collection called a *website*, which consists of a group of related web pages published on a topic by an organization or individual. Companies and individuals create websites to organize their related pages.

Pages and sites on the Web have some common characteristics:

➠ **Unique addresses,** which are formally called *URLs* (URL stands for Uniform Resource Locator, in case you're ever on *Jeopardy!*).

➠ **Connecting links** that move you from page to page when you select them. These *links* (also called *hypertext links* or *hyperlinks*) often appear underlined and blue. Pictures and other graphic images can also be links to other pages. Exploring the Web using links is easier than typing URLs.

In this chapter, you use Microsoft Internet Explorer to browse the Web. To get the most out of browsing, you juggle multiple sites at once. You find out how to search for almost anything, and you also use the Reader app for certain types of documents frequently found on the Web.

Browse the Web with Microsoft Internet Explorer

1. Open Internet Explorer by selecting its tile on the Start screen. Note the *command bar* at the bottom of the screen in **Figure 6-1**. The address for the current page, if any, appears in the command bar, located at the bottom of the screen. In **Figure 6-1**, the address is www.bing.com. Your screen may look different.

 Each time you open Internet Explorer, you see the default page, called the *home page*, or the page you were browsing last. You may see an error message if you're not connected to the Internet. If so, see Chapter 4 for information on connecting.

2. Select the address box in the command bar. A panel slides up to display tiles under *Frequent* and *Pinned*. You may not see anything under the headings until you browse some sites.

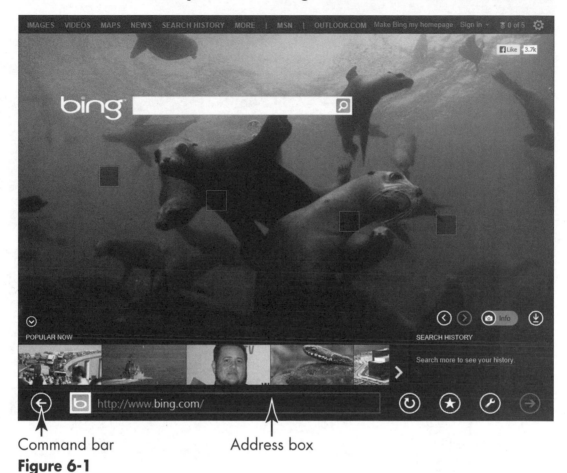

Command bar   Address box

Figure 6-1

 The tiles under *Frequent* and *Pinned* make it easy to return to web pages by simply selecting the tile you want. These tiles become more useful as you continue to browse. Eventually, you have to scroll to the right to see those that don't fit on the first screen.

3. In the address box, type `www.dummies.com` and select the go arrow (right-pointing arrow) or press Enter. The web page for the Dummies Press appears, as shown in **Figure 6-2**.

 If you don't have a keyboard, see Chapter 1 for information on using the virtual keyboard.

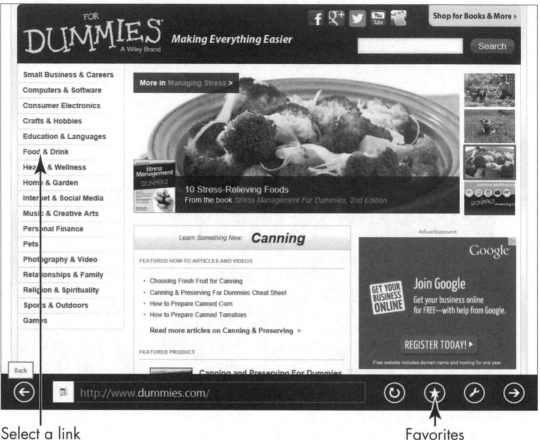

Select a link   Favorites

Figure 6-2

4. Select a link on the left side of the page (for example, select Computers & Software) with a click or a tap.

 To use the keyboard to select a link, press the Tab key until the link is selected, and then press Enter. (Seeing when the link is selected can be difficult.) I include other keystrokes as you need them.

5. Select the back arrow in the command bar (or press Alt+left arrow) to return to the preceding page. If you see a back arrow on the left side of the screen, you can select that instead.

6. Select the forward arrow (or press Alt+right arrow) to return to the page you visited in Step 4. If you see a forward arrow on the right side of the screen, you can use that instead. The browser remembers the pages you visit to make it easy to go forward and back.

7. Select the address box. The Frequent screen appears, as shown in **Figure 6-3.** Select the Bing tile. If you don't see that tile, type **www.bing.com** and press Enter to return to the Bing web page.

 Browsing the Web consists of entering addresses, following links, going forward and back, and using the Frequent tiles. Relatively simple activities that can absorb hours.

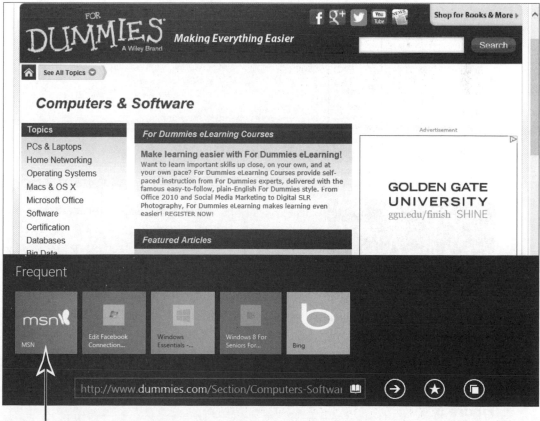

Frequently browsed pages

Figure 6-3

8. Select the Favorites button to the right of the address (refer to **Figure 6-2**). The command bar shown in **Figure 6-4** appears. Select the Pin Site button and then the Pin to Start button.

 You can change the text in the box before you select Pin to Start. However, there's usually no need to change the text unless it's overly long or unclear.

9. Return to the Start screen. Scroll to the right to locate the new tile for the Bing web page. Select that tile to open the page in Internet Explorer (IE).

10. Select the address box. (If you don't see it, right-click the screen to display the address box.) Note the tile for the Bing web page is also under the Frequent heading.

Enter text

Pin Site

Figure 6-4

Pin the pages you want to visit easily. See Chapter 2 for information on unpinning and rearranging the tiles on the Start screen.

11. To print this or any other web page, display the charms bar and then select the Devices charm. In the Devices panel, select Print, and then select a printer or select anything outside the Devices panel to cancel. For information on installing (and using) a printer, see Chapter 13.

 Some web pages are quite long, requiring more than one page of paper. Be certain you want to print.

12. Return to the Start screen.

 You may encounter web pages that don't open properly in the Windows 8 version of IE because it doesn't support every function found on web pages. See the section "Use Internet Explorer on the Desktop" for information on an alternative for viewing web pages.

Open Multiple Pages in Separate Tabs

1. Select the Internet Explorer tile on the Start screen.

2. Go to the Bing website at www.bing.com.

3. Display the command bar in **Figure 6-5** using one of these methods:

- **Mouse:** Click the right mouse button, making sure the pointer is not over a link, photo, or video.

- **Touchscreen:** Drag down from the top edge or up from the bottom edge.

- **Keyboard:** Press ■+Z.

Figure 6-5

 Use one of these methods if the command bar along the bottom disappears, as it will while you browse a page.

4. In the command bar, select the plus sign. On the next screen, select any tile or type a new page address.

5. Display the app bar again. Note two (or more) thumbnails at the bottom of the screen (see **Figure 6-6**). These thumbnails are called *tabs*, because older web browsers display notebook-like tabs instead of thumbnails. Select the first thumbnail tab to switch back to the first web page.

 Browsing in multiple tabs allows you to keep one page open while visiting another, perhaps to compare information or to follow a different thought.

Figure 6-6

 The keyboard shortcut for switching between tabs is Ctrl+Tab.

6. Once again, display the app bar. Select the X in the lower-right corner of one of the thumbnails to close that particular tab. Close as many open tabs as you want to reduce clutter and to simplify switching between open tabs.

 The keyboard shortcut for closing the current tab is Ctrl+W. (*W*? Long story.)

 When you switch to the Start screen, the pages you are browsing remain open in IE. When you switch back to IE, those pages are ready to use. To start IE fresh without any open pages, close each open tab.

Search for Anything

1. With Internet Explorer open, select the address box and then type **travel**. IE attempts to match what you type with a tile for a page you have browsed. (Ignore these matching tiles for this exercise, but take advantage of them later.) Select the go arrow next to the address box or press Enter.

 You can search the Internet from the Start screen without opening Internet Explorer. On the Start screen, type a search term. The Search panel opens with the search term you entered in the Search box and search topics listed below. Select a topic to open the Search app, which shows thumbnail Web pages pertaining to your search term. Select a Web page thumbnail to open a page in Internet Explorer.

2. A search results page appears, as shown in **Figure 6-7**. The results come from www.bing.com, which is the default search engine for IE. A *search engine* is simply a website that provides links to Web pages that match your search. (That definition, however, ignores the complex process going on behind the scenes.)

 Although you don't have to browse www.bing.com to begin a search, you should browse that page eventually to see the beautiful photos, which change daily (refer to **Figure 6-1**).

3. Scroll down the page of search results. Select any link you want to follow. If you get to the bottom of the page, select Next to see more search results.

Search results

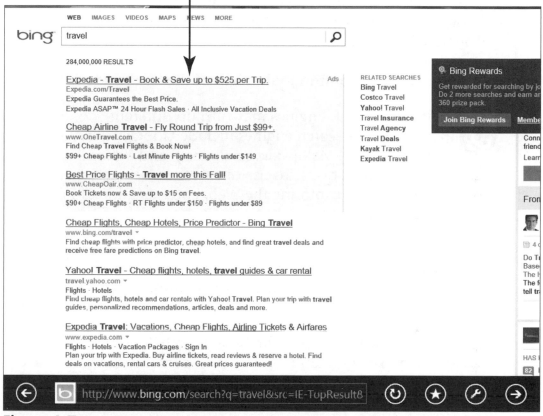

Figure 6-7

4. Return to the search screen using one of the following methods:

- Select the back arrow (or press Alt+left arrow) to return to the previous page. The more pages you've browsed one after another, the less effective the back arrow is in returning to the first page.

- Select the address box. Then either select the Bing tile (if there is one) or type **bing** and select Bing from the matching tiles. The more complex your search, the less effective this method because you have to perform the search repeatedly.

5. Select the search box at the top of the Bing page. After the word *travel*, type **new mexico** (no capitals needed). As you type, potential matches for your terms appear directly below the box. If you see an item matching the search you want, select the item. Otherwise, select the magnifying glass button to the right of the box to search.

 Different search engines may turn up different results. Other search engines include Google (www.google.com), Ask (www.ask.com), and Yahoo! (www.yahoo.com). To use one of these search engines when exploring the Web, enter its address in the address box.

 Search results often include links to suggestions for related searches and a history of recent searches you've made. Take advantage of anything that requires less typing.

6. Note the tabs at the top of the Bing page, below the search box. The first tab is Web, which contains the results you see by default. Additional tabs vary with the search. Select each of the tabs, which may include any of the following:

- **Images** displays pictures matching your terms.

- **Videos** displays clips and snippets related to your search terms.

- **Maps** will help you get there.

- **News** displays search results from recent news, instead of all the results of the broader Web.

- **More** leads to shopping and services Bing provides, as well as some information on using Bing.

The Images tab includes the SafeSearch setting, near the top of the page. Your options are Moderate, which attempts to filter out potentially offensive or obscene images, Strict, for even more filtering, and Off, for anything goes.

7. Close IE with one of the following techniques:

- **Mouse:** Move the pointer to the top of the screen until the pointer becomes a hand. Then click and drag IE off the bottom of the screen.

- **Touchscreen:** Swipe from the top edge and drag IE off the bottom of the screen.

- **Keyboard:** Press Alt+F4.

Closing IE or any other app is optional.

Work with the Reader App

1. On the Start screen, select the Internet Explorer tile.

2. Select the address box. (Right-click the screen to display the address box if you don't see it.) Then type **goo.gl/ yrgz** in the address box and press Enter. (That odd address is a shortened URL. I'm using it to demonstrate how to read PDF Web pages with the Reader app.) You see the message shown in **Figure 6-8** at the bottom of the page: *Do you want to open or save fw4.pdf from irs.gov?*

Select Open to view the document in Reader

Figure 6-8

3. Select Open. The Reader app opens with the contents of the linked document (in a format called PDF). Adobe Acrobat Reader is a program more commonly used to open these documents on computers other than Windows 8.1.

 Select Save (refer to **Figure 6-8**) if you want to read this document again. By saving the document to your computer, you can open it anytime, without returning to the web page.

4. In Reader, display the app bar, which is shown in **Figure 6-9**. Select the Two Pages button to display two pages at once. Select One Page to see just one page at a time. Continuous (the default option) displays the largest size text and less than one page at a time. Use one of the following methods to display the app bar in any app:

- **Mouse:** Click the right mouse button.

- **Touchscreen:** Swipe down from the top or up from the bottom of the screen.

- **Keyboard:** Press ⊞+Z.

Reader app bar

Figure 6-9

5. In the Reader app bar, select Find, which enables you to search a document for text. Type **dependent** and then select the magnifying glass or press the Enter key. Every instance of matching text is highlighted, as shown in **Figure 6-10**. Select Next or Previous to move through the document. Select Results to display a list of matching items in context (useful for long documents). Select Close to end the search.

To find text in a document, type here...and select here

Figure 6-10

6. Display the app bar again, and then select Save As. The Files screen appears. Keep or change the filename at the bottom of the screen. Select Save. Saving the document allows you to access it later without browsing the original web page.

 When saving any file, you can select the Files heading for a list of specific locations. If you see SkyDrive, select that to store this file in the cloud (on the Web) and automatically copy it to any linked computers.

7. Display the app bar one more time, and then select More, which displays the following functions:

- **Rotate** is useful if the document is not rotated correctly.

- **Info** displays information about the document, including who created it and when, as well as the document length. Permissions indicate what functions are available, most importantly printing.

8. To print this document, display the charms bar and then select the Devices charm. In the Devices panel, select Print, and then select your printer. Select the Print button to print or select anything outside the Devices panel to cancel. For information on installing (and using) a printer, see Chapter 13.

 Some documents are quite long, requiring more than one page of paper. Be certain you want to print.

9. Close the Reader app with one of the following techniques:

- **Mouse:** Move the pointer to the top of the screen until the pointer becomes a hand. Then click and drag IE off the bottom of the screen.

- **Touchscreen:** Swipe from the top edge and drag IE off the bottom of the screen.

- **Keyboard:** Press Alt+F4.

Change Microsoft Internet Explorer Settings

1. In Microsoft Internet Explorer, display the charms bar and then select Settings.

2. In the Settings panel for Internet Explorer, select the Options function at the top.

3. In the Options panel (see **Figure 6-11**) turn on Always Show Address Bar and Tabs if you want these items to always appear. (You don't have to display the Command bar to see them.)

Figure 6-11

4. In the Zoom section, select a spot in the bar. The farther left you select, the more of the page you see and the smaller the text. The farther to the right you select, the less of the page you see and the larger the contents. Notice the changes to the page you were on when you started these steps. Zoom to 120% for improved ease of reading. Select the back arrow at the top of the Settings panel.

5. On any web page, use one of these methods to change the zoom level:

- **Mouse:** Press the Ctrl key while rolling the mouse wheel away and back, which zooms in and then out.

- **Touchscreen:** Touch two fingers on the screen. Spread your fingers to zoom in. Pinch your fingers to zoom out.

- **Keyboard:** Press Ctrl+plus sign to zoom in. Press Ctrl+minus sign to zoom out. Press Ctrl+0 (zero) to return to normal (usually 100 percent).

These methods are independent of the Zoom setting you chose in Step 4, which sets the default zoom level for all pages.

6. In the Home Pages section, select the Customize button to open the Home Pages panel. Starting here, you can choose the home page that appears when you start the Internet Explorer app. Either enter the address of the page that you want or go to the page, revisit the Home Pages panel, and select the Add Current Site button.

Use Internet Explorer on the Desktop

1. On the Start screen, select the Internet Explorer tile. Select the address box. On the Command bar, select the Favorites button. If there is one, select the Bing tile (or type **www.bing.com** and then select the go arrow).

2. In the command bar at the bottom of the screen, select the page tools (wrench) button to display the menu choices shown in **Figure 6-12**.

Get app for this site

Find on page

View in the desktop

View downloads

http://www.bing.com/

Figure 6-12

 The Find on Page function enables you to type text to search for on the current page.

3. Select View in the Desktop to open the current page in the desktop version of IE, as shown in **Figure 6-13**. See Chapter 5 for help on working with the desktop.

 The desktop version of IE has more functions than the Windows 8 version, including a function called Favorites for organizing your most-visited web pages into folders. Desktop IE also enables you to install more functions called accelerators and add-ons, such as Adobe Reader (for printed documents and forms). If a page refuses to open or looks wrong in the IE app, see if using View on the Desktop helps. Desktop IE may ask for your permission to open or download additional functions. Be careful. Don't accept just anything from any website.

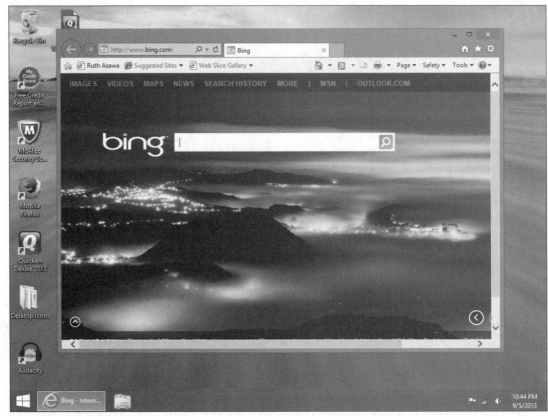

Figure 6-13

4. Examine the desktop version of IE, which is quite different from the IE app. The address bar at the top of the
window displays the web address for the page currently
shown in the browser. A tab appears to the right with the
title of the page.

5. Scroll the page using one of these methods:

- **Mouse:** Click in the scroll bar area on the right
  edge of the window. Or roll the mouse wheel
  toward you or away.

- **Touchscreen:** Drag the page up or down.

- **Keyboard:** Press Page Down or the spacebar. Scroll back up by pressing Page Up or Shift+spacebar. Use the up or down arrows to scroll up or down, respectively, one line at a time.

6. Click or tap to select a link.

 A web page may take some time to open. Look in the tab for indications of a delay, such as a *Wait* message or a rotating circle.

7. To return to the preceding page, select the back arrow to the left of the address bar or press Alt+left arrow or the Backspace key.

8. Select the forward arrow (or press Alt+right arrow) to return to the page you opened in Step 6. The browser remembers the pages you visit to make it easy to go forward and back.

9. Switch to the Start screen using one of the following methods:

- **Mouse:** Move the pointer to the lower-left corner of the screen, and then click.

- **Touchscreen:** Swipe from the right edge for the charms bar, and then tap the Start charm.

- **Keyboard:** Press the ■ key.

 You can use the desktop version of Internet Explorer also by selecting the Desktop tile on the Start screen. Then start Microsoft Internet Explorer (IE) by selecting the blue *e* icon in the taskbar at the bottom of the screen.

E-Mailing Family and Friends

Chapter 7

E-mail has largely replaced the notes and letters of previous centuries. Every day, billions of e-mail messages circle the globe, conveying greetings, news, jokes, even condolences.

E-mail also provides a way to send and receive *attachments*, such as documents or photos. Who needs faxes or postcards?

The Mail app gives you access to e-mail using your Microsoft account. A glance at the Start screen can tell you whether you have unread e-mail and if so, who it is from.

Your Microsoft account can be associated with an e-mail address from any e-mail service provider, including Microsoft's own Hotmail (www.hotmail.com), Live (www.live.com), Outlook (www.outlook.com), or Xbox (www.xbox.com). You can also use e-mail services such as Yahoo (www.yahoo.com) and Gmail (www.gmail.com) without having a Microsoft account. However, you have to access non–Microsoft account e-mail using a web browser or an app other than Microsoft's Mail app. See Chapter 6 for information on browsing the Web.

In this chapter, you use the Mail app for e-mail. You compose, format, and send e-mail, as well as respond to incoming e-mail.

 If you don't have a physical keyboard, see Chapter 1 for information on using the virtual keyboard.

Use the Mail App

1. For e-mail on Windows 8.1, select the Mail tile on the Start screen. If you are not currently signed in using a Microsoft account, enter your e-mail address and password on the Sign In screen that appears, and then select Sign In. (See Chapter 4 for information on creating a Microsoft account.)

2. The first time you use the Mail app, you may not see much, if you haven't used your Microsoft account for e-mail on another computer. Who would have written you already? You may, however, see a message or two from Microsoft.

3. On the Inbox screen, select the Folders button. The All Folders panel slides in from the left, as shown in **Figure 7-1**.

 If the screen resolution is high enough to allow more information on the screen, you may see the Mail panel and the Inbox panel side-by-side. At lower resolutions, these panels replace each other as you choose them.

All folders panel

Folders button

Figure 7-1

4. Select any of the following categories in the Mail panel, and then select the Folders button to return to the Mail panel:

- **Inbox:** E-mail you have received but not moved elsewhere appears here, including both read and unread e-mail.

- **Drafts:** As you compose e-mail (next section), you can save your message as a draft until you are ready to send it.

- **Sent:** Copies of the e-mail you send are stored here, appropriately.

- **Outbox:** When you send e-mail, it moves to the Outbox until it has been processed, which may be instantaneously. If you're not connected to the Internet, e-mail waits here until you establish a connection, and then it is sent.

- **Junk:** Messages are moved here — either automatically or by you — instead of the Inbox, if they are suspected of being, well, *junk*. The more common term for unwanted e-mail is *spam*. (It's a long story.) You may want to check this folder occasionally to see if a message was misfiled here.

- **Deleted:** Self-explanatory? You can move messages out of Deleted Items if you change your mind.

 As you switch categories, Mail syncs with the Web to display items in that category. You may not see anything other than *Syncing* or *Up to date* until you send and receive e-mail.

5. Proceed to the next section, "Write an E-Mail Message."

 You can say "send me e-mail," instead of "send me an e-mail message." I, for one, never say "send me *an* e-mail."

 After you've received some e-mail messages, you can search for specific messages by displaying the charms bar, selecting Search, and then selecting Mail and typing the content you're searching for in the search box, such as subject, sender, or something in the message. This process works anywhere — you don't have to be in the Mail app.

Write an E-Mail Message

1. To compose an e-mail message in the Mail app, select the New button (it looks like a plus sign) in the upper-right corner of the screen. (It doesn't matter which panel appears on the left.) The Compose screen appears, as shown in **Figure 7-2**.

Enter an e-mail address

To		
Cc		

More

[Draft] Add a subject

Add a message

Sent from Windows Mail

Figure 7-2

2. In the To box, type an e-mail address. (Feel free to write me using `markjusticehinton@hotmail.com`.) If the e-mail address is incomplete, it will be highlighted. Press the Tab key, touch the screen, or use the mouse to move to the next option.

 Instead of typing an address, you can open the People app (Windows 8.1's address book) by clicking the word To and selecting a name there, but you probably don't have any contacts at this time. See Chapter 8 for information on adding contacts to the People app.

 To send e-mail to more than one person at once, press Enter after you type an address and enter the next address. You can also enter an e-mail address in the CC box. (Once upon a time, CC stood for *carbon copy*, and then it became *courtesy copy*.) Technically, it makes no difference whether you use additional To addresses or the CC. To send a copy without revealing you've done so, select More, and then enter addresses in the BCC (*blind* or *blocked* CC).

3. Select the box that displays Add a Subject (that prompt disappears when you select the box). Enter a few words describing your message content or purpose. Using lowercase is fine.

4. Select below the Subject line. Type your message. Avoid all caps — purists consider caps to be SHOUTING! No need to press Enter as you approach the end of the line — this isn't a typewriter.

 Some people start a message with a salutation, such as *Hi, Mark*, but many people do not. Some people sign e-mail using their initials. E-mail can be as formal or casual as you choose to make it.

 Words underlined with a red squiggle aren't recognized by Windows 8.1 and may be misspelled. Right-click or tap and hold to see a pop-up list of suggested spellings. If the spelling is correct, use Add to Dictionary for words you use frequently or Ignore for those you don't.

5. When you're ready to send the message, select the Send button, which looks like an envelope. If you decide not to send the message, select the Delete button.

 E-mail you compose but haven't sent yet is kept in the Drafts folder. You can postpone writing a message and finish it later by going to the Drafts folder and opening your message there. To go the Drafts folder, select the Folders button and then select Drafts in the All Folders panel.

6. If you select the Send button, your message is sent and you return to the folder you were on at the beginning of Step 1.

7. Repeat from Step 1 as needed.

Format E-Mail

1. If you want to add bold, italics, even color to e-mail, select the text you want to fancy-up. If no text is selected, your formatting will apply to the word in which the *cursor* (the blinking vertical line in the content) is located.

- **Mouse:** Click and drag the mouse pointer over the text you want to select.

- **Touchscreen:** Tap and drag over the text you want to select.

- **Keyboard:** With the cursor at the beginning of the text you want to select, hold down the Shift key as you press the right or down arrow to select text. Release the Shift key only after you have completed your selection.

 To apply formatting to one word, double-click or double-tap that word to select it and display the app bar in one step.

 The keyboard shortcut to select all text is Ctrl+A. No mouse or touchscreen method is quite so complete.

2. The app bar appears as you make your selection, as shown in **Figure 7-3**. Select any of the following formatting options:

- **Font:** Choose a font by name and specify the size of the text. For example, the text in this book is Giovanni Book and the font size is 12.5. The older I get, the larger the font I use.

- **Text Color:** Choose from the colors that pop up when you select this option.

- **Highlight:** Choose from the colors that pop up to highlight text.

- **Bold:** Bold is used for emphasis to make text stand out.

- **Italic:** Although italic can also be used for emphasis, it may be harder to read than normal or bold text.

- **Underline:** Because links are usually underlined automatically, you may want to avoid underlining text that isn't a link.

- **List:** Choose Bulleted List or Numbered List on the pop up to create a list.

- **Emoticons:** This button opens a panel on the bottom of the screen. The top row of choices changes the *emoticons* (smiley faces and other small pictures or symbols) available in the panel. Choices are Recently Used, People and Faces, Activities, Food and Things, Travel, Nature, and Symbols. These options could keep you busy for days.

 See Chapter 1 for information on using the virtual keyboard's emoticons.

- **Hyperlink:** This button opens a dialog box so you can enter a web address and create a hyperlink. See Chapter 6 for more information about hyperlinks.

- **Open a New Window:** This button opens your e-mail message in its own window.

- **More:** This button displays four more options: Save Draft, Undo, Redo, and Clear Formatting.

 The keyboard shortcut for Undo is Ctrl+Z. For Redo, press Ctrl+Y.

Select text to format

Figure 7-3

 Click the Attachments button in the upper-right corner of the screen to open the *file picker*, which lets you select documents and photos to send along with your e-mail message. When the file picker appears, select a file to attach or select Go Up to navigate to other locations or apps, such as Camera and SkyDrive.

3. When you have finished formatting the text, select the Send button.

Read and Respond to Incoming E-Mail

1. On the Start screen, you may see an indication that you have received e-mail. Note that the Mail tile may display the following information:

- The large and wide tiles display the sender's address or name, the subject line, and a portion of each unread message in succession, as well as a count of unread messages.

- The medium and small tiles display the unread message count.

- The Mail tile doesn't display any information if the Live Tile option is off.

2. Select the Mail tile. The Mail app opens on the last screen you viewed — not on the specific message displayed on the live tile, if any.

3. If necessary, select the Folders button and then select Inbox in the All Folders panel. See the section "Use the Mail App" for the steps. Unread messages appear in bold.

4. Select a message under the Inbox heading. The content of that message appears to the right, as shown in **Figure 7-4**.

5. After you read the message, you can select one of the following options in the upper-right corner:

- The **Respond** button (with an arrow curving back on an envelope) creates a new message based on the current message.

- The **New** button (the plus sign) starts a new message to anyone.

- The **Delete** button (the trashcan) moves the e-mail from Inbox to Deleted Items.

Hotmail				

Inbox

All ⌄   🔍

☐ **Peter**
Dinner?   1:05 PM

Outlook Team
Welcome to your new Outlo...   Aug 15

Peter
Dinner?   Aug 15

Hotmail Member Services
Please sign in to your account   Aug 15

The SkyDrive Team
New features, tips and updat...   Aug 15

Hotmail Member Services
Please sign in to your account   Aug 15

The SkyDrive Team
New features, tips and updat...   Aug 15

Peter   9/9/2013 1:05 PM
to Jerry Talbert

Dinner?

Jerry--

Care to have dinner

--Peter

Figure 7-4

6. Select the Respond button, and then select Reply from
the list that appears. Reply starts a new message (refer to
Figure 7-2) in response to the selected message and
includes the text of the selected message. The subject line
is automatically *Re: [the original subject]*. You'll use this
option most often. Complete your message and select the
Send button.

In the Respond button list, Reply All sends your
response to all the other recipients, if a message is
addressed to more than one person. The Reply
option sends your response only to the sender. Select
Forward to send the selected message to someone
else. You can add your own text or remove portions
of the forwarded message in the process.

See the sections "Write an E-Mail Message" and
"Format E-Mail" for more information on composing
an e-mail message.

7. Select any message in the Inbox category. Display the Mail app bar by using a right-click, by swiping up or down, or by pressing ▦+Z. Note the following options:

- **Move:** Use this option to move the selected e-mail from one category on the left to another. For example, move a message to the Junk category or from Junk to Inbox, if it's a message you want. In the Mail panel, select the category to which you want to move the selected e-mail.

- **Sweep:** Use this option to delete several messages from the same sender. On the pop-up menu that appears, choose Delete All, Delete All Older than 10 Days, Delete All But the Latest.

- **Junk:** Use this option to move a message to the Junk folder.

- **Flag:** Use this option to place a flag icon next to the message in the Inbox so you remember to deal with the message later on.

- **Mark Unread:** Use this option if you want the message to appear unread (bold in Inbox). Some people do this with messages they want to deal with later.

- **Delete:** Use this option to delete the message.

- **More:** On the pop-up menu that appears when you select the More button, choose Sync to sync Mail with the Web. (Syncing is done automatically, but choose this option if you think Mail is out of sync.) Choose Print to print the e-mail message.

 If you add e-mail accounts from providers such as Gmail, you may see additional categories or options. See the section "Add an E-Mail Account to Mail" at the end of the chapter.

Send E-Mail from Other Apps

1. You can e-mail information from other apps, such as Internet Explorer and News. On the Start screen, select the Internet Explorer tile. See Chapter 6 for information on using the web browser.

2. On any web page, display the Share panel using one of the following methods:

- **Mouse:** Move the mouse pointer to the upper-right corner of the screen. On the charms bar, select the Share charm.

- **Touchscreen:** Swipe from the right edge of the screen, and then tap the Share charm.

- **Keyboard:** Press ▓+H (think *sHare*) to go straight to the Share panel.

3. On the Share panel, shown in **Figure 7-5,** select the Mail tile.

Figure 7-5

Mail isn't available for sharing with all apps. You won't know until you try.

4. The Mail panel slides in from the right, as shown in **Figure 7-6.** Enter an e-mail address under To. Enter a subject as well. A thumbnail image of the web page appears in the content area. You can add, delete, or change any of this. When you're ready to send the message, select the Send button.

← Mail ✉

Jerry Talbert
jinx257@hotmail.com ⌄

To [   ]

Windows 8 For Seniors For Dummies

Add a message

Windows 8 For Seniors For Dummies

Welcome, Readers March 28, 2013: Please read Windows 8 App Updates for Readers before updating your Windows 8 apps. Windows 8 For Seniors For Dummies will available from Amazon and bookstores by October, 2012. Regardless of the reader's age, this book...

http://www.mjhinton.com/help/?page_id=1521

Sent from Windows Mail

Figure 7-6

Curiously, formatting options aren't available in this panel, except as keyboard shortcuts such as Ctrl+B for bold, Ctrl+I for italic, and Ctrl+U for underline. Repeating the keyboard shortcut removes the formatting. The Delete and Save to Drafts options are also missing here. To cancel this e-mail, select the back arrow next to Mail or select anywhere outside the panel.

 The next time you use the Share panel in Internet Explorer or another app that shares with Mail, the e-mail address you used in Step 4 appears near the top of the panel. Select that address to save time in sharing something else with that person.

Change Mail Settings

1. In Mail, display the Settings panel, shown in **Figure** 7-7. Then select Accounts.

Mail app access multiple e-mail accounts

Figure 7-7

2. On the Accounts panel, select your e-mail account at the top of the panel. Note these settings, which are shown in **Figure 7-8**:

Enter text to automatically add e-mail

Figure 7-8

- **Account Name:** The name of the e-mail service provider. You can change this, if you want. I might use *Mark's e-mail.*

- **Download New E-mail:** If you don't want e-mail constantly streaming into Inbox, you can change this setting to every 15 or 30 minutes, Hourly, or Manual, in which case use the Sync button on the Mail app bar to check your mail.

- **Download E-mail From:** You can limit how far back to download messages to your computer. This setting isn't relevant in a new e-mail account.

- **Content to Sync:** Understandably, you want to sync e-mail between your service provider and your computer. However, you may see options to sync Contacts, Calendar, or other information between the service provider and your computer. Generally, you want everything in sync.

- **Show E-mail Notifications:** Turn on this setting to see pop-up notifications when new e-mail arrives.

- **Automatically Download External Images:** By default, Mail downloads images attached to or embedded in e-mail messages. Turn off this option to avoid downloading images, if you're paying for your Internet connection by the minute or byte.

- **Use an E-mail Signature:** Mail automatically inserts *Sent from Windows Mail* into each message. Enter text here that you want automatically inserted at the end of your message. For example, I use *peace, mjh* as my e-mail signature. If you don't want any text inserted automatically, select the switch under this option to change it from Yes to No.

- **Preferred E-mail Address:** This setting is a reminder of your e-mail address.

- **Password:** Enter the password of your e-mail account here so you don't have to enter it each time you collect e-mail from the account.

Add an E-Mail Account to Mail

1. If you have another e-mail address, you can add it to Mail. For example, follow these steps to add an existing Gmail account to Mail. In Mail, display the Settings panel (refer to **Figure 7-7**) and then select Accounts.

2. In the Accounts panel, select Add an Account.

 Many people have more than one e-mail address. Your Internet service provider probably gave you an e-mail account and you may have another through work or school. However, this feature isn't for everyone.

3. In the Add an Account panel, select the service with which you have an e-mail account. If your service doesn't appear here, select Other Account. If you have a Gmail address (or you just want to see what's next), select Google.

4. On the Add Your Google Account screen, enter your Gmail address and password in the appropriate boxes. Then select Connect. Select Cancel if you don't want to continue.

5. You may see the message *Connecting to a service.* You then enter your Gmail address and password again and select the Accept button.

6. Select the Accounts button (in the lower-left corner of the screen). A pop-up menu lists your e-mail accounts in alphabetical order, as shown in **Figure 7-9.** A number next to each account name shows the number of unread messages in the account. You can switch to a different account by selecting an account on the pop-up menu.

Switch between accounts

Figure 7-9

See the preceding section, "Change Mail Settings," for the steps to review or change settings for your newly added account.

Staying in Touch with People

Chapter 8

*T*he Web brings people together in many ways beyond e-mail. Long ago, paleo-nerds hunkered in bulletin board systems, precursors to today's forums. *Social networks* are digital neighborhoods where your neighbors include family, friends, colleagues — maybe even your real neighbors. We use social networks to *share* the information or entertainment we discover and to post *status updates*, short declarations of the moment, such as *I'm feeling particularly eloquent today*.

Unlike the broader Web, these social networks are gated communities that require an account name and password for full access. This suggestion of privacy and security, however, shouldn't be completely trusted. If nothing else, the networks themselves are watching you.

A few social networks are worth noting here: Facebook, Twitter, and Flickr. You find out more about these and others shortly. For now, realize that each social network is a separate website with its own way of doing things, requiring some mental adjustment as you move between them. Furthermore, how a site works may change from one visit to the next, often to the dismay of participants.

Get ready to . . .

Moreover, with so many people posting so many thoughts, links, and likes, keeping up becomes a problem. The People app comes to your rescue by pulling in contact information, status updates, and more from several services at once. Use the People app as your address book and as a window on what everyone is doing without having to navigate through each network's website.

In this chapter, you add contacts to the People app, both manually and by connecting to Facebook or another service. You make your most important contacts stand out by pinning them to the Start screen or marking them as *favorites*, for prominence in the People app. You use the Calendar app to keep track of birthdays, anniversaries, appointments, and other events.

This chapter also shows you how to have face-to-face video chats with Skype. In a video chat, you see the person to whom you're speaking on your computer screen as you talk with them, and your chat friend sees you, too. I remember when video chatting was strictly for science fiction films.

Explore the Social Networks

If you don't have an account with Facebook or another social network, you can create an account through the People app. However, I recommend that you go to a service's website to create a new account, and then use your new account name and password in the People app.

➡ **Facebook** (www.facebook.com) is the epitome of social networks. You know about Facebook already, unless you've been living in a cave. (These days, even caves have Internet connections.) Billions of people and organizations have Facebook accounts and *pages*. Facebook popularized the verbification of *friend* (bow your head for the late *befriend*), as well as the use of *like* as a mere acknowledgment, a tip of the hat, if you will. (The less popular *hat tip* or *ht* is a favorite among *bloggers*, digital journal-keepers who stand apart from the collective.) Somehow *poke* as a greeting hasn't gained the same traction as other new usages.

➡ **Twitter** (www.twitter.com) pares communication down to short status updates (*tweets*) in an endless stream of text messages. Twitter is favored by professional journalists and bumper-sticker fans.

➡ **LinkedIn** (www.linkedin.com) is popular among professionals seeking business contacts (and jobs) more than casual social interaction.

➡ **Flickr** (www.flickr.com) is older than the upstarts and immensely popular among photographers and lovers of photography.

➡ **Pinterest** (www.pinterest.com) has quickly collected enthusiasts who share images in shifting mosaics.

➡ **MySpace** (www.myspace.com) lost the race to Facebook and serves as a reminder that, like empires, social networks do not endure. It is our need to connect that endures.

Add Contacts to the People App

1. On the Start screen, select the People app.

2. If you haven't signed in already using your Microsoft account, the Sign In screen appears. Enter your Microsoft account e-mail address and password, and then select Sign In.

 You need a Microsoft account to use Mail, Calendar, and People. When you sign in to one, you're signed in to all three apps. See Chapter 4 for information on creating a Microsoft account.

3. What you see first in People depends on whether the app found contact information associated with your Microsoft account. You may see familiar names or an invitation to connect to other services. For now, add one new contact manually. (You connect to other services later.) Display the New Contact screen by selecting the New Contact button on the People app bar (see **Figure 8-1**), using one of the following methods:

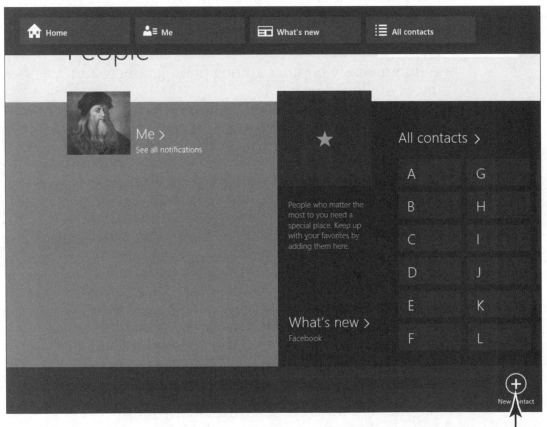

Select New Contact to add someone to your address book

Figure 8-1

- **Mouse:** Click the right mouse button. Click the New Contact button, which sports a plus sign.

- **Touchscreen:** Swipe down from the top or up from the bottom of the screen. Tap New Contact (the plus sign).

- **Keyboard:** Press ■+Z. If necessary, press the Tab key until New Contact (the plus sign) is highlighted, and then press the Enter key.

4. Much of the information on the New Contact screen (shown in **Figure 8-2**) is optional. Enter the information that you want access to throughout Windows 8.1, not just in the People app. (For example, think about what you want to access in Mail.) You can enter any person's name and information you want, but let me suggest the following:

- **Account:** Ultimately, you may link multiple accounts using the People app. Which account do you want this new contact associated with? For now, only one option may be available.

- **First Name: Mark**.

- **Last Name: Hinton**.

- **Company: PC Training & Consulting**.

- **Email: markjusticehinton@hotmail.com**. (Select Personal and choose Work from the pop-up list.)

- **Phone:** (Leave phone blank for me.) Select Mobile and note the many categories for phone numbers.

Enter just the information you want

New contact

Account

Sbcglobal ▾

Name

First name

Mark

Last name

Hinton

Company

PC Training & Consulting

⊕ Name

Email

Personal ⌄

markjusticehinton@hotmail.com ✕

⊕ Email

Phone

Mobile ⌄

⊕ Phone

Address

⊕ Address

Other info

⊕ Other info

Figure 8-2

5. Note the following buttons with plus signs. Select each in turn to see the available options. Add data as you want:

- **Name:** You can add a middle name (**Justice**), nick-name (**mjh**), title (**Computerist**), as well as several other names.

- **Email:** Add up to two more e-mail addresses.

- **Phone:** Add up to seven more phone numbers!

- **Address:** Add up to three mailing addresses.

- **Other Info:** Options include Job Title (**Author**), Significant Other (**Merri**), Website (**www.win-8mjh.com**), and Notes, a box for free-form notes.

6. When you're done, select Save to add this contact (or select Cancel to throw away the new contact). The added contact appears on-screen, as shown in **Figure 8-3**.

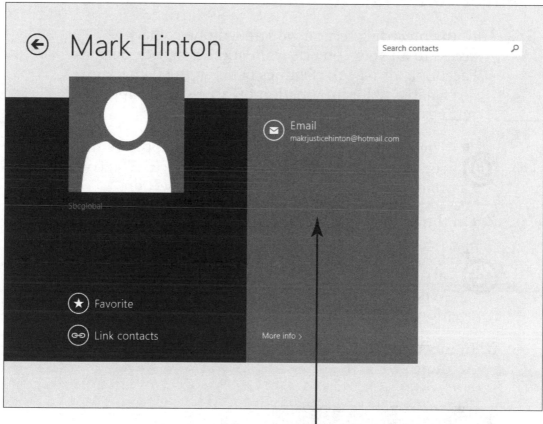

Information on the contact card

Figure 8-3

7. Select People in the app bar or select the back arrow.

 The photo associated with a contact is usually selected by the contact as part of his or her profile on a specific network. The generic image in **Figure 8-3** may change as you connect to social networks.

Connect to Social Networks

1. In the preceding section, you added one contact. For access to all your contacts from another service, such as Facebook, display the Settings panel in the People app. See Chapter 2 for information on accessing an app's settings.

 The very first time you use the People app, you may see an option to connect to other services. You could start there and jump to Step 4 in this section.

2. On the Settings panel, select Accounts.

 For an account you've already added, select that account in the Accounts panel to configure what data Windows 8.1 downloads and how frequently the downloads occur.

3. In the Accounts panel (see **Figure 8-4**), select Add an Account.

Figure 8-4

4. In the Add an Account panel, select Facebook, unless you don't have a Facebook account. (Let me shake your hand, you rare creature.) You can choose another service, in which case the steps will be similar but the screens will be different.

5. The screen briefly displays *Connecting to a Service*, and then the Connect screen appears. If you see What Else Happens When I Connect, select that option to read everything that will happen, as shown in **Figure 8-5**.

 Understandably, most people are concerned about privacy. We don't know fully the effect of linking all our activity on the Web.

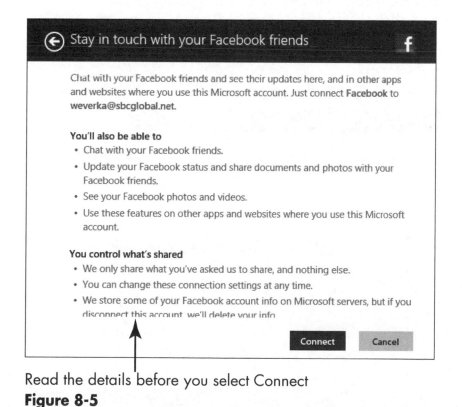

Read the details before you select Connect

Figure 8-5

6. Select the Connect button. Or select Cancel, if you prefer.

7. On the Connecting screen, shown in **Figure 8-6,** enter your e-mail address and password (or other account information for the selected service). Select Keep Me Logged In or Remember Me for convenience. Then select the Log In or Authorize button. (The wording of buttons varies with the service but the underlying choice is Yes or No.)

Wow! When you sign in to Facebook, the screen says, "Microsoft would like to access your birthday, work history, current city, photos, videos, website and your friends' birthdays, work histories, current cities, photos, videos, and websites." This sounds kind of scary. And you have to click OK to keep going.

Enter your account information

Figure 8-6

8. The service you're connecting to may display additional forms or information. When you log in to Facebook, you are asked whether you want to share your personal information on Facebook and your friends' information with Microsoft. Click OK twice.

9. As the final screen says, you're ready to go. Select Done.

10. After the People app synchronizes with your added service, the People screen displays all your contacts, including those from the added service.

 Look for small logos in the lower-right corner of the People screen; these logos indicate to which services the People app is connected. For example, an *M* indicates Microsoft and an *f* indicates Facebook.

 The What's New category on the app bar displays combined updates from people on your connected services, much as you would see on your home page for each service.

Catch Up with People

1. In the People app, select one of your contacts from the People screen.

 On the People screen, select a letter or type a name in the Search box. Selecting a letter scrolls the contact list to names with the letter you selected. After you type a name, press Enter or select the magnifying glass button to search. Matches appear on the left. Select the person whose contact details you want.

2. The contact screen for the selected person appears, as shown in **Figure 8-7**. That person's name and profile photo (or a generic silhouette) appear. Note the following information may appear:

- **Email:** Select this option to send e-mail (the screen switches to the Mail app) or a message through the service from the People app.

- **Call Home:** Select this option to video chat with the contact on Skype (see "Chat Face-to-Face with Skype" for more information).

- **Map:** If an address is part of the contact details, select this option to see the location of that address in the Map app.

- **View Profile:** View the contact's service Profile in the web browser (in this case, the contact's Facebook page).

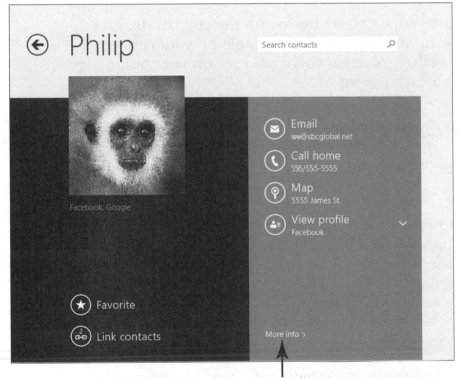

Select an option or scroll right to see more

Figure 8-7

When you write an e-mail message in the Mail app, you can select recipients from your contacts, instead of manually entering e-mail addresses. See Chapter 7 for information on writing e-mail.

3. Scroll to the right to see additional information, such as the What's New (also called status updates) and Photos sections.

 This contact screen is more than static data. You are looking at the information you would see on the service's own web pages. You can even interact, adding comments and *likes* (the Facebook term for a thumbs-up, or a vote of approval).

 Much like the contact details screen, the Me item on the People home screen displays your profile photo, a link to your profile, as well as the updates you've posted, notifications from contacts, and your online photos.

4. To make this contact easier to access, display the app bar on the contact screen, and then select Pin to Start. The Pin to Start box appears, as shown in **Figure 8-8.** Change the text or not. Select the Pin to Start button.

Philip

Pin to Start

Pin to Start   Edit

Figure 8-8

5. Switch to the Start screen. Scroll to the right to see the tile for the contact you pinned. This live tile displays the contact's profile photo alternating with recent status updates.

 See Chapter 2 for information on arranging tiles on the Start screen.

6. Select the contact tile you just pinned. (If necessary, open the People app and select the contact again.) Display the app bar again. Note that the option now reads Unpin from Start.

7. Select Favorite. The app bar disappears. Return to the People screen by redisplaying the app bar and selecting Home. On the People screen, contacts you flag using Favorite appear first, with larger tiles. (You can have as many favorites as you choose.) Select the favorite contact to return to the contact's main screen.

8. Display the app bar for the contact again. Select Edit. The Edit Contact Info screen appears and is largely the same as the New Contact screen (refer to **Figure 8-2**). Select Cancel, unless you change information that you want to save.

 Use the Link option to consolidate separate contacts. For example, your friend may end up in People as two separate contacts from two separate services. Link the two contacts.

 To delete a contact from a connected service, you must go to the website for that service, such as www.facebook.com, and delete the contact there. When the People app syncs with the service, the contact will disappear from the app.

Add a Birthday or Anniversary to the Calendar

1. To see the calendar and add events, open the Calendar app from the Start screen. You may see events and appointments from services you connected to in People or Mail. Display the app bar, as shown in **Figure 8-9**, by right-clicking, by swiping up or down, or by pressing ⊞+Z.

Change views using the Calendar app bar

| | What's next | | Day | | Work week | | Week |

Sunday	Monday	Tuesday	Wednesday	Thursday	Friday	Saturday
27	28	29	30	31 Halloween	1	2
3	4	5	6	7	8 Dennis Wever... / Lunch wit... 11AM	9
10	11 Veterans Day	12	13 Dentist Ap... 9AM	14	15	16
17	18	19 Wedding Anni...	20	21	22	23
24	25	26	27	28	29	30

Sync   New

Figure 8-9

2. On the Calendar app bar, select each of the following, formats, redisplaying the app bar each time:

- **What's Next:** This format lists upcoming events and holidays.

- **Day:** This format displays two days side by side (initially, *Today* and *Tomorrow*), with a box for each hour. Select arrows near the top of the screen to scroll back or forward one day at a time. Scroll up and down to see more hours in the day.

- **Work Week:** This work week (Monday through Friday) appears. As with the Day format, scroll up and down to see different hours and use the arrows to move forward or back a week at a time.

- **Week:** *This week* appears. Scroll or use the arrows to go from hour to hour or week to week.

- **Month:** The current month appears in the classic month layout (depending on the size of your screen, you may have to scroll to see this format). Today is highlighted with a different color. Use arrows near the top to move forward and back a month at a time.

3. To create a new event, select any date in the month (or select any hour in the Day or Week formats). Then select the New button in the app bar. The Details screen appears, as shown in **Figure 8-10.**

4. Change any of the following data for an event:

- **When:** Select the month, day, and year from pop-up lists.

- **Start:** Select the hour, minute, and AM or PM from pop-up lists.

Peter's calendar
weverka@sbcglobal.net

Lunch with Mom

When

| November | ⌄ | 05 Tuesday | ⌄ | 2013 | ⌄ |

Add a message

Start

| 12 | ⌄ | 30 | ⌄ | PM | ⌄ |

How long

| 90 minutes | ⌄ |

Where

| Her favorite restaurant |

Show more

Add information for an event

Figure 8-10

- **How Long:** For standard blocks of time, select from 0 Minutes, 30 Minutes, 1 hour, 90 Minutes, or 2 Hours. Select All Day for events that don't have a specific start and stop time. For an end time with the same options as Start, select Custom, and then make an appropriate selection — use this option for multiday events, such as a vacation.

- **Where:** The location of the event, either in general (*downtown*, for example) or a specific location name or address.

 Select Show More for additional options.

- **How Often:** Most events occur once. However, you can select Every Day, Weekday, Week, Month, or Year to create a recurring event, such as a birthday or an anniversary.

- **Reminder:** How far in advance of the event do you want Calendar to display a notification? Choose None, 5 Minutes, 15 Minutes, 30 Minutes, 1 Hour, 1 Day, 18 Hours, or 1 Week.

- **Status:** Use this option if you share your calendar with someone, such as a receptionist, who may schedule you for other events.

- **Who:** Enter one or more e-mail addresses. A copy of the event details will be e-mailed to these addresses. Use Who in lieu of the Share charm.

- **Private:** Select this option to prevent this event from appearing on a shared or public calendar. The event remains visible on your own screen.

5. On the right side of the details screen, enter the event name above the line. Add an optional message or note below the line.

6. When you're done, select the Save button. Select the Cancel button (the arrow in the upper-left corner of the screen) if you don't want to create an event.

7. On the calendar, your event appears on the specified date and time.

8. To edit an event, select it on the calendar. The Details screen opens. Add or change any detail.

 To delete an event, edit it, then select the Delete button (a trash can). If you added the event through a different service, you may have to return to that service to delete the event.

If your Microsoft account is connected to services such as Facebook and Gmail, events from those services appear on your calendar. Display the Settings panel, and then select Accounts to add or remove connected accounts. Display the Settings panel, and then select Options to show or hide connected calendars and to specify different colors for different calendars' events.

Tweak PC Settings for Social Apps

1. Change how the apps in this chapter let you know what's going on. On any screen, display the charms bar, and then select Change PC Settings to open the PC Settings app.

 See Chapter 3 for information about the PC Settings options.

2. Select PC and Devices on the left, and then scroll down the right side to the Lock Screen Apps section, as shown in **Figure 8-11**.

Figure 8-11

3. Some apps can display information on the Lock screen. This information can be brief (in the first row of icons) or detailed (the last icon). In **Figure 8-11**, the first three icons represent Mail, Weather, and Calendar. Three more positions are available, as represented by the plus signs. To add a fourth app, select one of the plus signs. To change one of the current apps, select its icon. In either case, the Choose an App pop-up appears listing all apps capable of displaying summary information. For example, Mails display the number of unread messages for each app. Select the app you want from the pop-up, for example, Weather. If you don't want any app in that particular position, select Don't Show Quick Status Here (*here* means this specific position). You can modify any or all of these positions.

4. In the same section, the second row contains a single button that you use for an app for which you want to display more detail. For example, if you choose the Calendar app, your next appointment and all-day events will appear on the Lock screen. Select the icon, and then select the app you want from the Choose an App pop-up. If you don't want any detailed information on the Lock screen, select Don't Show Detailed Status on the Lock Screen.

5. Return to the Start screen.

Chat Face-to-Face with Skype

1. On the Start screen, select the Skype app. You can use this app to video chat with others. To use Skype, your computer must have audio and video capability. You can also use Skype if a webcam is connected to your computer.

You need a Microsoft account to use Skype. See Chapter 4 for information about creating a Microsoft account.

 The easiest way to make calls through Skype is to enter the names of the people you want to call on your Contacts list in the People app. See "Add Contacts to the People App" earlier in this chapter.

2. The first time you use the Skype app, the screen displays *Can Skype use your webcam and microphone?* Select Allow to continue. (If you don't want to continue, don't choose Block unless you *never* expect to use the Skype app. Instead, simply switch back to Start.)

3. If you haven't signed in already using your Microsoft account, the Sign In screens appear. You are asked to enter your current password (if you started Windows 8.1 with a local password), your Microsoft account e-mail address and password, and a security code from Microsoft.

4. Select I'm New to Skype. (If you've used Skype before, select I Have a Skype Account and skip to Step 5.) Then agree to the terms of use and click Next.

5. The Skype screen lists the names of people on your Contacts list (from the People app) and people you have called before using Skype. You can select one of these people to call them now. If the person you want to call isn't listed, select the Search button (which looks like a magnifying glass). The Search screen opens, as shown in **Figure 8-12**. Enter a name and select the Search button (or press Enter). If the name still doesn't appear in the search results, select the Search Directory button. The Skype Directory opens. Scroll to find the person you want to call, using the person's photo ID and geographical information as your guide.

Enter a name

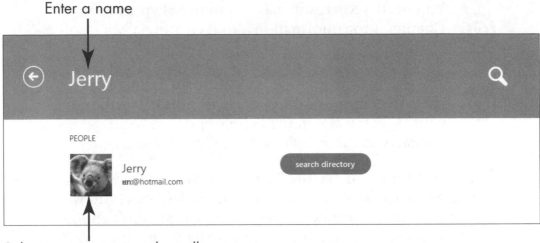

PEOPLE

Jerry
jerry@hotmail.com

search directory

Select a name to start the call
Figure 8-12

6. When you see the name of the person you want to call, select the name. Then, on the call screen, select the Video button, as shown in **Figure 8-13**. You hear a ring tone as the call is made, and you see the person's face if he or she answers, as in **Figure 8-14**. Your face appears in the lower-right corner of the screen so you can see what your face looks like to the caller. Start talking. Smile. Trade the latest news. Have a ball.

 Select Video and Audio buttons when you need a little privacy. Select the Video button to turn off your video (the other caller can't see you); select the Microphone button to turn off your audio (the other caller can't hear you).

Start the call

Figure 8-13

 Select the Options button and choose Instant
Message on the pop-up menu to send an instant
message to the other caller. In the message panel
(refer to **Figure 8-14**), type your message and press
Enter. Sending text messages is a useful way to communicate when you have technical difficulties or the
other caller isn't answering. You can also send URLs
by instant message. Select the Options button and
choose Instant Message on the pop-up menu again to
close the Instant Message panel.

7. Select the red Hang Up button to complete your call.

Turn off video or audio   Options   Hang up   Instant messages

Figure 8-14

8. When someone calls you, the Incoming Call panel appears, as shown in **Figure 8-15**. Select the Video button to initiate the call.

Select Video to receive a call

Figure 8-15

Part III
Having Fun with Windows 8.1

Visit www.dummies.com/extras/windows8dot1forseniors for help getting a family photo set up as your lock screen background.

Installing Apps from the Microsoft Store

Chapter 9

You can do many things with Windows 8.1, such as sending e-mail, browsing the Web, playing games, and looking at photos and videos. You can read the news and chat with family and friends. All these functions and more involve computer programs. Back in the day, such programs were called *applications*. Now, we call them *apps*.

Windows 8.1 comes with a few apps installed, such as the Weather and Travel apps. (See Chapter 2 for information on using these two apps and apps in general.) To obtain other apps — free or otherwise — you use the Microsoft Store.

To install an app from the Microsoft Store, you need a Microsoft account. See Chapter 4 for information on setting up a Microsoft account.

Microsoft tests and approves all apps in the Microsoft Store. For quality and security reasons, you can install Windows 8.1 apps only from the Microsoft Store.

In this chapter, you peruse the apps in the Microsoft Store, including those already installed on a new machine. You update existing apps, install a new one, and find out how to uninstall an app. Finally, you set up a payment method in case you want to buy an app.

Stroll Through the Microsoft Store

1. On the Start screen, select the Store tile, which looks like a shopping bag with handles and the Windows logo, as shown in **Figure 9-1**.

Microsoft Store tile

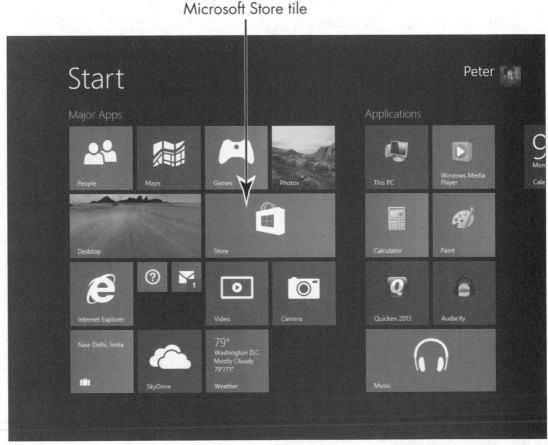

Figure 9-1

2. Look over the Store home screen (see **Figure 9-2**). The Store is organized into categories that stretch off the right side of your screen, so scroll the screen right to see more.

 To scroll with a mouse, roll the wheel or click the bottom of the screen. To scroll on a touchscreen, tap and then drag your finger from right to left or left to right. To use the keyboard to scroll, press the Page Down or Page Up keys. You can also use the Tab key to jump between sections or the right and left arrow keys to move through the screen one item at a time.

Microsoft Store home screen

Figure 9-2

3. Right-click to display the app bar and note the following category headings:

- **Picks for You:** Examine apps that Microsoft thinks will interest you based on your history of downloading apps.

- **Top Paid:** Check out apps that have the highest average rating among apps you have to pay for.

- **Top Free:** Check out apps that have the highest average rating among free apps.

- **New Releases:** See apps recently added to the Store.

- **Popular Now:** Find out which apps are most popular with other shoppers at the Store.

- **Games:** Play card games, solve puzzles and word games, and more.

- **Social:** Connect to friends and family.

- **Entertainment:** Check out apps that don't fit the other categories, such as those for drawing.

- **Photo:** View, edit, and share photos.

- **Music & Video:** Listen to music and watch movies.

- **Sports:** Follow your favorite sport or team. (Yeah, cricket!)

- **Books & Reference:** Read and research.

- **News & Weather:** Keep current.

- **Health & Fitness:** Want to get in shape? Start by computing.

- **Food & Dining:** Locate eateries, as well as rate and review restaurants.

- **Lifestyle:** If you think entertainment is a vaguely defined category, check out lifestyle.

- **Shopping:** Put the world's catalogues at your fingertips.

- **Travel:** Get you there and back.

- **Finance:** Manage the money you don't spend on other apps.

- **Productivity:** Send e-mail and create schedules.

- **Tools:** Manage your computer.

- **Security:** Keep your computer and data safe.

- **Business:** Analyze business data.

- **Education:** Study the stars, languages, or piano, or prep for the SAT.

- **Government:** Learn more about the government and its workings.

You may see other categories, as well.

 Is the app you want a game or entertainment? Will it make you productive or is it a tool? The category to which an app is assigned is determined by the app developer. In some cases, it's not clear why an app is in one category and not another. So it goes.

4. To return to the Store home screen from any other store screen, use one of the following methods:

- **Mouse:** With the mouse pointer in an empty area, click the right mouse button to display the app bar. Click Home.

- **Touchscreen:** Swipe down from the top or up from the bottom to display the app bar. Tap Home.

- **Keyboard:** Press +Z. Press the Enter key or the spacebar.

The back arrow in the upper left of most screens takes you back one screen. Click this arrow to retrace your steps through the Store.

Explore Available Apps by Category

1. On the Start screen, select the Store app.

2. On the Store home screen, right-click to display the app bar, and then select the Games category. The Games page appears, displaying tiles for various games.

3. In the Games category, scroll to the right and select the See All category. You see a screen similar to the one in **Figure 9-3.** From the See All category, you can search for games by subcategory, price, and other criteria.

Search using criteria

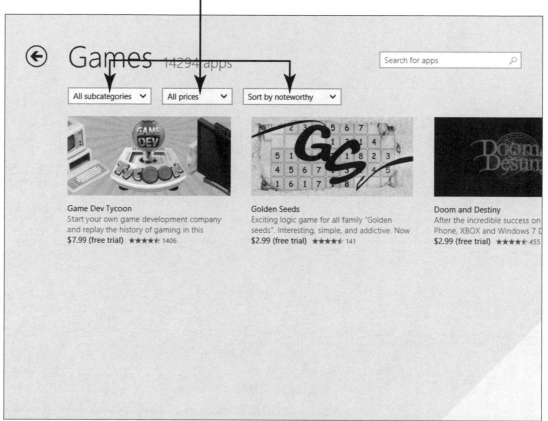

Figure 9-3

4. Select All Subcategories and choose the Puzzle subcategory to display just puzzles.

 As you make selections in Steps 4–6, the apps matching selections appear automatically.

5. Select All Prices and then choose Free. (Trial apps are free
for a trial period or a number of uses before you have to
pay before continuing to use them.)

6. Select the Sort By drop-down box and then choose Sort
by Highest Rating. The screen shown in **Figure 9-4**
appears.

Back arrow

Figure 9-4

 Use these steps to explore any app category.

7. Select the Mahjong Deluxe Free tile.

 If you don't see the Mahjong Deluxe Free tile, go to the next section, "Search for an App by Name."

8. Proceed to the "Install a New App" section, or return to the Store home screen.

Search for an App by Name

1. On any Store screen, click in the Search for Apps box. This box is in the upper-right corner of the screen.

2. Type *mahjong* in the Search for Apps box. As you type, potential matches appear below the box, as shown in **Figure 9-5.** If you see Mahjong Deluxe Free, select it in the Search panel. (Don't select the paid version at this time.)

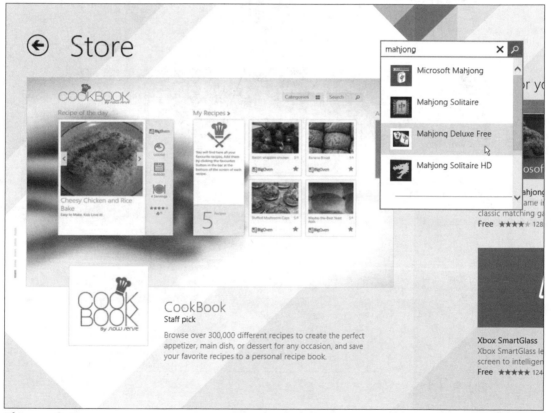

Figure 9-5

> **3.** If you don't see Mahjong Deluxe below the search box, press the Enter key to search further. Select the app from the Results screen, as shown in **Figure 9-6**.

> **4.** Proceed to the next section, "Install a New App," or return to the Store home screen.

Type search text here

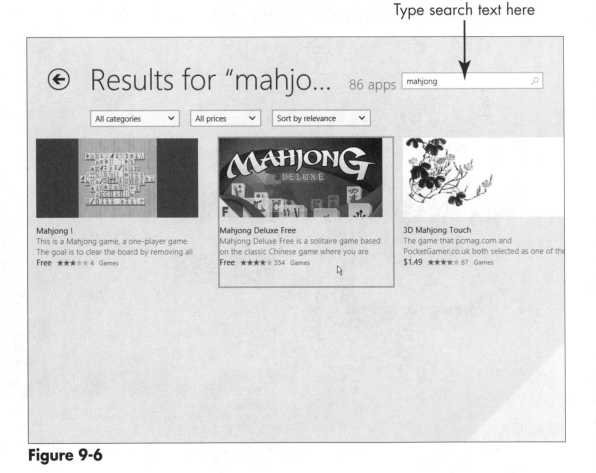

Figure 9-6

Install a New App

1. In the Store, display the Mahjong Deluxe Free screen. (See the section "Search for an App by Name" for details.)

2. The screen shown in **Figure 9-7** appears. This (and any) app screen has lots of information. Start at the top:

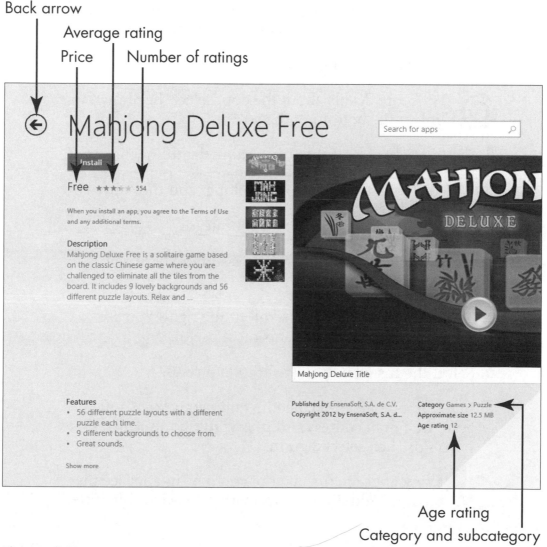

Back arrow

Average rating

Price   Number of ratings

Age rating

Category and subcategory

Figure 9-7

The back arrow (left-pointing arrow in a circle) next to the game's name takes you back to the previously viewed screen.

3. On the left side of the screen, note the following:

- The Install button (don't click it just yet)

- The cost of the app

- The average rating in stars (5 stars is the best) and the number of times the app has been rated

- The Terms of Use link

For more details about the app, select the Show More link at the bottom of the screen.

4. On the right side of the screen, note the following:

- The name of the app developer and the copyright

- The app's category and subcategory

- Age rating, which indicates suitability or age appropriateness

5. To view reviews by users, scroll to the right. You see reviews that Microsoft deems most useful.

6. Select the Install button (refer to **Figure 9-7**).

7. If you're not already signed in, enter your Microsoft account e-mail address and password on the screen that pops up. Then select Sign In.

Many apps are free. Before you buy an app, see the section "Add Billing Information to Microsoft Store."

If you purchase an app, you are buying a license to install that app on up to five machines using the same Microsoft account. The Microsoft Store will track how many times and on which machine the app is installed.

8. You may see *Installing Mahjong Deluxe Free* in the upper-right corner of the screen. When installation is complete, a brief notification appears on any screen you are viewing. You may also hear a beep.

 Installing an app may take a few seconds or a few minutes. You can do anything while an app installs — except use the app.

9. Display the Mahjong Deluxe Free screen again. In **Figure 9-8**, note that *Last updated on this PC* is followed by a date. This notice tells you when the app was installed on your computer.

 If you don't see *Last updated on this PC*, the app may still be installing. If after a few minutes, you still don't see this message, select the Install button again.

10. To play Mahjong Deluxe Free or to use any app after you install it, return to the Start screen and then go to the Apps screen. To get to the Apps screen from the Start screen, click the downward-pointing arrow.

11. On the Apps screen, apps are listed in alphabetical order. If you haven't used an app yet, the word *New* appears beside its name, as shown in **Figure 9-9**. Find the new tile for the app you installed (you may have to scroll right) and select that tile to open the app.

This message tells you when the app was installed

Figure 9-8

 To play Mahjong Deluxe Free, select the play button (the right-pointing triangle). Select Green Dragon to play. Choose the first game. Select uncovered tiles with matching symbols from any of the stacks on screen to remove pairs of tiles. Have fun!

 You can move the Mahjong Deluxe tile to the Start screen. See Chapter 2 for information on rearranging tiles on the Start screen.

Look for the word New next to recently installed apps

Figure 9-9

Examine Your Apps

1. To see which apps you have, display the app bar on any Store screen, using one of the following methods:

- **Mouse:** With the mouse pointer in an empty area, click the right mouse button.

- **Touchscreen:** Swipe down from the top or up from the bottom.

- **Keyboard:** Press ⊞+Z.

Open the first drop-down menu and choose All Apps to see all your apps on the Your Apps screen.

2. In the app bar that appears at the top of the screen, select Your Apps.

Use Home on the app bar to return to the Store home screen any time.

3. If you see a Sign In button, select that button and enter your Microsoft account e-mail and password on the next screen.

4. On the screen shown in **Figure 9-10**, scroll to see which apps you have. Each tile displays an icon, the app name, and the purchase date (even for free apps). Lastly, each tile indicates *Installed* or *Not installed.*

⊕ Your apps 21 apps

Hearts (Free)	Windows Alarms	Finance
Purchased 8/13/2013	Purchased 8/12/2013	Purchased 7/17/2013
Installed	Installed	Installed

Mahjong Deluxe Free	Windows Calculator	Games
Purchased 8/13/2013	Purchased 8/12/2013	Purchased 7/17/2013
Installed	Installed	Installed

Bing Food & Drink	Windows Reading List	Mail, Calendar, and Peop
Purchased 8/12/2013	Purchased 8/12/2013	Purchased 7/17/2013
Installed	Installed	Installed

Bing Health & Fitness	Windows Scan	Maps
Purchased 8/12/2013	Purchased 8/12/2013	Purchased 7/17/2013
Installed	Installed	Installed

Help & Tips	Windows Sound Recorder	Music
Purchased 8/12/2013	Purchased 8/12/2013	Purchased 7/17/2013
Installed	Installed	Installed

Clear

Figure 9-10

How can you have an app you haven't installed? If you sign into more than one computer using your Microsoft account, you might install an app on one machine but not another.

5. Select the Apps Not Installed on this PC box. If you have signed in to more than one computer with your Microsoft account, each computer is listed separately here, enabling you to see just those apps installed on a selected computer. (This option is irrelevant if you use only one computer.)

6. Select the Sort By box. As you install more apps, you may find it useful to Sort by Date or Sort by Name.

7. Select one of your installed apps. You can view details for the selected app, as described in the preceding section.

8. Return to the Store home screen using the back arrow or the Home button on the app bar.

Update Installed Apps

1. To check for updates to your installed apps, display the settings options (shown in **Figure 9-11**) from any Store screen as follows:

- **Mouse:** Move the pointer to the lower-right corner of the screen to display the charms bar, and then select the Settings charm.

- **Touchscreen:** Swipe from the right side to display the charms bar, and then select the Settings charm.

- **Keyboard:** Press ⊞+I to go directly to the settings options.

Figure 9-11

 The Store tile on the Start screen displays the number of apps that have updates available, if any. If you don't see *Updates* in the upper right of any store screen, your apps are all up-to-date.

2. In the Settings panel, select App Updates.

3. On the App Updates screen, note that updates are automatically downloaded. This saves time when you decide to install updates. Select Check for Updates.

4. On the next screen, if you see *No updates available*, you're done. Return to the Store home screen.

5. When an app has an update available, the app tile is automatically selected, as indicated by the check mark. If you don't want a particular app updated at this time, select its tile to remove the check mark. If you decide to update the app later, simply select the tile again to add the check mark.

 Installing all available updates at once is easier than picking and choosing apps to update.

6. Select the Install button. You return automatically to the Store home screen (or whichever screen you were on when you selected the Updates option). The installation process happens quickly, so you may not see the *Installing updates* message in the upper-right corner.

 Updates install *in the background*, meaning you can do anything, including leaving the Store app, during the installation.

Rate and Review an App

1. On the Apps screen, select the Mahjong Deluxe app. If you don't have this app, see the section "Install a New App" or substitute any app you have installed.

2. Display the Settings panel for the app you have on-screen. Select Rate and Review.

 Every app has a Rate and Review option under Settings. You can also select Write a Review on the details screen for that app in the Microsoft Store.

 You can rate or review only apps you've installed, and you must be signed in with your Microsoft account. To rate or review a preinstalled app, install the app to associate the app with your Microsoft account.

3. The Write a Review screen appears, as shown in **Figure 9-12**. Select the number of stars you want to give this app. (Select the first star on the left for the lowest rating up to the last star on the right for the highest rating.)

 If you want to rate the app but not review it, select Cancel. Select the star rating on the app screen (refer to **Figure 9-8**).

4. In the Title box, type a summary or overview of your comments, such as **Great app** or **Needs work**.

5. In the Review box, say what you will, up to 500 characters, including spaces and punctuation. Be helpful, if possible. Select the Submit button when you're done with your review (or Cancel to abandon your review).

Write a review

Mahjong Deluxe Free

Rating

★ ★ ★ ★ ★

Review – optional

Title

Comments

0/1000

Note: The name and picture for the Microsoft account you use with the Store will be posted with your review.

Submit   Cancel

Figure 9-12

Your comments may help another person decide whether or not to install an app. In addition, the app's developer may use customer feedback to fix problems or add features.

 Your Microsoft account name and picture — but not your e-mail address — appear with your review.

6. On the app screen in Store, the option Update Your Review replaces Write a Review and your rating appears instead of the average rating. Your review will appear on the Reviews screen after some delay. You can update a review later, if your rating or comments change, but you can't retract or delete a review.

Uninstall an App

1. On the Apps screen, locate Mahjong Deluxe or another app you want to remove from your computer. Use one of the following methods to select the app to uninstall:

- **Mouse:** Place the pointer over the app tile, and right-click (click the right mouse button) to display the app bar. Then click the Uninstall button.

- **Touchscreen:** Swipe down or up slightly on the app tile to select it without opening or moving it. The app bar is displayed. Tap the Uninstall button.

- **Keyboard:** Press the arrow keys to highlight the app, and then press the spacebar to select the app without opening it. Press ⊞+Z to display the app bar, use the arrow keys to highlight Uninstall, and then press the spacebar to begin the process.

2. A message appears to tell you that the app will be removed from your PC, as shown in **Figure 9-13.** (To cancel, click or tap anywhere outside the box.) To delete the app, select the Uninstall button. If you change your mind later, you can reinstall the app from the Store.

Uninstall the selected app

Figure 9-13

Add Billing Information to Microsoft Store

1. To add the billing information necessary to buy apps, select the Store tile on the Start screen. In the Store, display the Settings panel using one of these methods:

- **Mouse**: Move the mouse pointer into the lower-right corner to display the Charms bar. Click the Settings charm.

- **Touchscreen**: Swipe from the right edge. Tap the Settings charm.

- **Keyboard**: Press ■+I to go directly to the Settings panel.

2. In the Settings panel, select Your Account.

3. If you see Sign in to Windows Store, select the Sign In button. On the next screen, enter the e-mail address and password associated with your Microsoft Account. See Chapter 4 for information on creating a Microsoft account.

4. On the Your Account screen, note the e-mail address. If this is not the account to which you want to add payment information, select Change User or Sign Out and enter the correct e-mail address and password.

5. Select Add Payment Method. The Payment and Billing screen appears, as shown in **Figure 9-14**.

← Payment and billing

Choose a payment method
New payment method

◉ Credit card

○ PayPal

Add payment information

Credit card type *

◉ VISA   ○ [MASTERCARD]   ○ [AMERICAN EXPRESS]   ○ [DISCOVER]

Credit card number *

- Enter without dashes or spaces -

Expiration date *

MM ∨   YYYY ∨

Name on card *

CVV *

What's this?

[TRUSTe CERTIFIED PRIVACY]

Figure 9-14

6. Under Choose a Payment Method, select Credit Card.

 PayPal is a payment service. See www.paypal.com for information on creating a PayPal account.

7. In the Add Payment Information section, do the following:

- Select your credit card type.

 You must fill out all parts of this form except for Address Line 2.

- Enter your credit card number in the box provided. Don't enter dashes or spaces.

- Under Expiration Date, select the month (MM) and year (YYYY) your card expires.

- Enter your name as it appears on your credit card.

- Under CVV, enter the three- or four-digit verification code from your credit card. (Select What's This? for an illustration of the location of this code on your card.)

8. In the Billing Address section, do the following:

- Enter your street address, city, state, and zip code.

- Select your Country/region.

- Under Phone Number, enter your area code in the first box and the remainder of your number in the second box.

9. When you are ready to continue, select Submit.

10. If any of your data is incomplete or invalid, the form remains on screen. Look for indications of a problem. Review each entry before selecting Submit.

11. If your information was accepted, you return to the Your Account screen. Under Payment and billing info, note your credit card type, the last four digits of your number, and the expiration date.

12. To change, add, or view your credit card information, select Edit Payment Method. On the Payment and Billing screen, you can edit card information (except for type and number). You can also choose a new payment method.

 Use the View Billing History link to open billing information in the web browser.

Your payment and billing information is associated with your Microsoft account. Any machine you sign in to using your Microsoft account can be used to make purchases. For added security, select Yes under Always Ask for Your Password When Buying an App.

13. Select the back arrow to return to the Store. You can select Buy on any app information screen. See the section "Install a New App."

Taking Photos and More

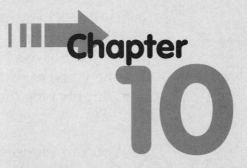

Windows 8.1 makes enjoying digital photos easy. You can pick and choose photos to look at or display a group of photos in a slide show. Make a favorite photo your Lock screen background so you see it every time you start Windows 8.1. In this chapter, you do all these things.

If you have a printer, you can print photos for yourself or to send to someone. Even black-and-white prints of color photos may be nice.

Of course, if you want to take your own photos, nothing beats having a digital camera. Copy photos from your camera to your Pictures folder for viewing and sharing. Or use the Camera app with the built-in camera found in many laptops and tablets.

In this chapter, you use the tools that come with Windows 8.1 for working with and editing photos. You may want the additional features of a digital photo organizer and editing program. You might want to check out my book *Digital Photography For Seniors For Dummies* (Wiley Publishing, Inc.) for detailed steps on organizing, editing, printing, and sharing photos as well as on using a digital camera.

Take Photos (and Videos) with Your Computer

1. Select the Camera app on the Start screen. If you don't have a webcam, the app screen displays *Connect a camera.* If you don't have a built-in webcam or the resolution of the one you have is too low, you can easily add a webcam. Simply plug the camera into your computer — it's that easy.

 You can choose from many good webcam models. Generally, get the highest video resolution you can afford, because you'll probably use the camera for video chats. Consider the size of the camera, its attachment to your computer, and whether or not it has a microphone (you want a mic).

2. The first time you use the Camera app, the screen displays *Can Camera use your webcam and microphone?* Select Allow to continue. (If you don't want to continue, don't choose Block unless you never expect to use this app. Instead, simply switch back to Start.)

3. The Camera app opens, and there's a good chance you recognize the face staring back at you. Very likely the face isn't wearing dark glasses like the debonair guy in **Figure 10-1.** To take a photo, smile and then click or tap the Camera button or anywhere on the image. You may hear a shutter click. Your photo is placed automatically in a folder called Camera Roll in the Pictures folder.

4. If you see Change Camera in the app bar, select that option. Many tablets and laptops have two cameras, one that faces you and one that points in the opposite direction. Switch to the camera away from you when you want to use your computer for something other than a self portrait. Take another picture — they're free. Select Change Camera again to switch back to see yourself.

Shoot a video

Take a picture

Figure 10-1

5. In the app bar, select Exposure and drag the slider up and down. The Exposure setting determines the balance between light and shadow in photos. Try experimenting with different exposures to present yourself in the best possible light.

6. In the app bar, select Timer. Nothing happens until you click or tap the screen, at which point a countdown timer appears, giving you three seconds to compose yourself. Select Timer again to turn off this feature.

7. Select the Video button (refer to **Figure 10-1**). Nothing happens until you click or tap the screen, at which point you're in moving pictures. A counter indicates the length of the video. Short is sweet in video. You can speak, too. Click or tap the screen to stop the video. Like photos you take with the Camera app, videos are saved initially in the Camera Roll subfolder of the Pictures folder. Select the Video button again to turn off the video function and return to taking still photos (with the next click or tap).

8. Return to the Start screen. See the section "View Photos" to see the photos you just took.

Copy Photos from Your Camera

1. If your camera came with a cable, connect that cable to the camera, and then connect the other end of the cable to a USB port on your computer. If your laptop or tablet has a built-in card slot, you can take the memory card out of the camera and insert it in that slot.

 If your computer doesn't have a built-in card slot, consider buying a small memory card reader that plugs into your computer and works with your camera's memory card. You don't need a multicard reader, just a reader with a single slot the size of your camera card. I consider a card reader more convenient than using a cable.

2. Windows 8.1 detects your camera or its memory card and may briefly display a notification indicating *Tap to choose what happens with memory cards.* (You can also click the notification.) If you're quick enough to tap or click the first notification, Windows 8.1 displays your choices, as shown in **Figure 10-2**. Select Import Photos and Videos, if that option is available, and then skip to Step 4. If you don't catch the notification in time, continue to Step 3 to import photos another way.

Select the Photos app

Canon PowerShot ELPH 100...

Choose what to do with this device.

Open device to view files
File Explorer

Import photos and videos
Photos

Take no action

Figure 10-2

 See Chapter 3 for information on increasing the time a notification remains on-screen.

3. Start the Photos app, and then display the app bar by right-clicking, by swiping down or up, or by pressing ■+Z. Select the Import button. No need for lightning reflexes. If you see more than one removable disk listed, your card is probably *D:*. If you choose the wrong disk, you'll recognize that fact in the next step, and you can repeat this step with a different disk.

4. Your photos appear on the Removable Disk screen, as shown in **Figure 10-3.** The photos you select on this screen will be imported to your Pictures folder, to a sub-folder named after today's date. To import all photos, select the Select All button. If you don't want all the photos, select the ones you want. A notice at the bottom of the screen tells you how many photos (and videos, if you shot those) you have selected. When you're ready to import the photos, select the Import button.

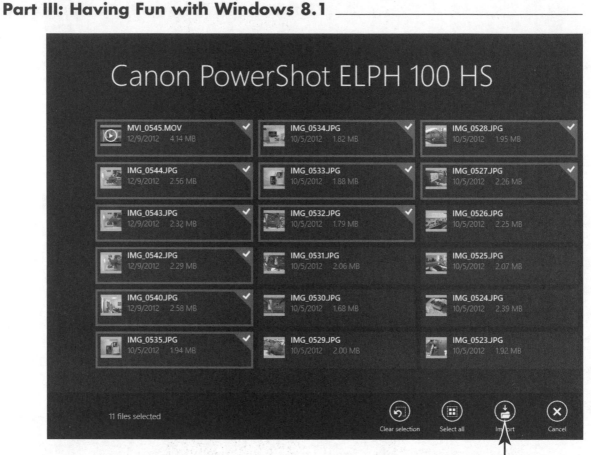

Select the Import button

Figure 10-3

 Organizing photos can be a challenge. If you dump
more than a few dozen photos into the Pictures
folder without using folders, finding a specific photo
later will be difficult. Using folders with unintelligi-
ble names doesn't help, either. Most of my folder
names are based on the year and month (such as
2013-06) or the subject, such as Luke the
Lovehound.

5. A notice in the upper-right corner of the screen tells you how many pictures are being imported, and then you see your pictures in the Photos app, as shown in **Figure** 10-4. The top of the screen shows the name of the subfolder on your computer where the photos were copied. This subfolder is located in the Pictures folder.

Figure 10-4

If the photos on your memory card don't import automatically the next time you copy photos, you can tell Windows 8.1 how to handle memory cards. On the Start screen, type **autoplay**. In the Search panel, select Settings. In the Results screen, select AutoPlay Settings. The AutoPlay window opens on the desktop. In the Camera section, select Import Photos and Videos (Photos) on the drop-down menu. Switch back to the Start screen. Remove your memory card or disconnect the camera cable. Reinsert or reconnect. This method for changing AutoPlay may be helpful for other media types or devices.

View Photos

1. To see photos on your computer, select the Photos app on the Start screen. The Photos home screen opens, as shown in **Figure 10-5.** It shows the contents of the Pictures folder on your computer. Subfolders in the Pictures folder appear on the left. Your screen will look different.

2. If you don't see any pictures, skip to one of the following sections:

- If you have a digital camera, see "Copy Photos from Your Camera."

- If your computer has a built-in camera or a webcam, see "Take Photos (and Videos) with Your Computer."

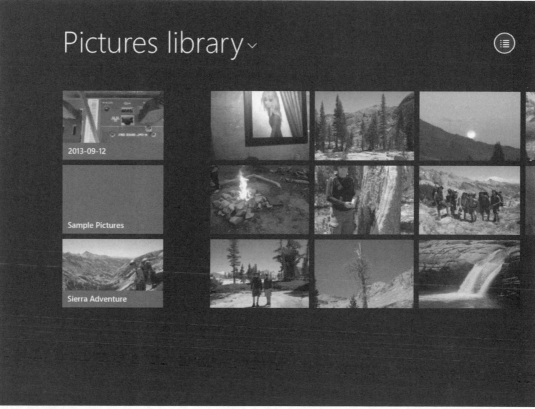

Figure 10-5

3. If you see pictures in your Pictures folder, scroll to the right to see more photos.

 You can take a screenshot — a picture of the current screen — by pressing ■+Print Screen. (A touchscreen or mouse equivalent is not available.) The screen dims slightly to indicate the capture, which is stored automatically in the Screenshots folder in your Pictures folder. Use this technique to create your own documentation of problems or something you want to see again later.

4. If necessary, select a folder in your Pictures folder (folders appear first, followed by photos). Scroll to the right through your photos. Select any photo to see it full screen. (Due to proportions, the photo may fill only the width or the height, not both.) Scroll through the full-screen photos by selecting an arrow on the left or right side of the screen or by clicking or tapping the right edge of the screen (to go forward) or the left edge (to go back). Press the PageDown key (forward) or PageUp key (back).

5. Display the app bar, as shown in **Figure 10-6.** Select the Slide Show button. The photos appear full screen in succession. Stop the slide show by selecting a photo or by displaying the app bar again. Use the back arrow to return to the folder.

 Select the button in the upper-right corner of the screen to switch between Thumbnails and Details view. In Details view, you can see each photo's name, when it was taken, and its file size.

6. Select one of your photos to display it full screen.

7. Zoom in and out on a photo using one of these methods (repeat to zoom in or out more):

- **Mouse:** Click the plus sign in the lower-right corner to zoom in. (Ignore the charms bar, if it appears.) Click the minus sign to zoom out.

- **Touchscreen:** Touch two fingers on the screen. Move your fingers apart to zoom in. Pinch your fingers closer together to zoom out.

- **Keyboard:** Press Ctrl+plus sign (actually, press the equals sign — no need to press the Shift key) to zoom in. Press Ctrl+minus sign to zoom out.

 Zoom in to see part of a photo made larger.

| Delete | Open with | Set as | Slide show | | Rotate | Crop | Edit |

Figure 10-6

8. Display the app bar. Select the Set As button and note the following options, using any or all if you want:

- **Lock Screen:** Set one of your own photos as the one that appears on the Lock screen.

- **Photos Tile:** By default, the Photos app tile displays a photo from your Pictures folder. If you prefer, you can set a single photo as the one on the Photos app tile.

Use the Delete button in the app bar to delete a photo. You can select more than one photo by using a right mouse-click or a tap and drag. After you select Delete, a pop-up box lists how many photos will be deleted. Select the Delete button to delete the photos, or press Esc if you change your mind about deleting. See Chapter 14 for information on undeleting files.

 The Photos app offers many options for editing photos. See the section "Edit Photos Using the Photos App."

Share Photos by E-Mail

1. In the Photos app, select one of your photos.

 You can select more than one photo to e-mail by right-clicking or by using a finger to drag down slightly on additional photos. Clear individual selections by repeating the process or use Clear Selection to deselect all.

2. Display the Share panel using one of the following methods:

- **Mouse:** Move the mouse pointer to the upper-right corner of the screen. On the charms bar, select the Share charm.

- **Touchscreen:** Swipe from the right edge of the screen. Tap the Share charm.

- **Keyboard:** Press ■+H (think *sHare*) to go straight to the Share panel.

3. On the Share panel, select the Mail tile. (The number of selected photos appears in the Share panel.)

 You can share using any apps that appear in the Share panel.

4. The Mail panel slides in from the right, as shown in **Figure 10-7.** Enter an e-mail address under To. Add a subject. A thumbnail image of the selected image appears in the content area. You can add a message below the photo. When you're ready, select the Send button in the upper-right corner. The Mail panel indicates *Sending email.*

Send button

Pictures lib

Mail

Jerry
jinx@hotmail.com ⌄

To

3 items

3 files attached ⌃

Sent from Windows Mail

Sierra Adventure

Delete   Copy   Cut

Figure 10-7

The next time you use the Share panel in Internet Explorer or another app that shares with Mail, the e-mail address you used in Step 4 appears near the top of the panel. Select that address to save time when sharing something else with that person.

Print Photos Using the Photos App

1. In the Photos app, select one photo using a click or tap for full-screen viewing.

2. Display the charms bar, and then select Devices.

3. Select Print. A list of printers appears, as shown in **Figure 10-8.** Select your printer.

Select your printer

Figure 10-8

 If you have a printer but it doesn't appear in the list, you may not have selected a photo or you may have two or more photos selected. As this book goes to press, the Photos app doesn't have an option for printing more than one photo at a time.

4. Select a printer. The Printer panel expands into view, as shown in **Figure 10-9.** Note the preview. Select the Print button. (To cancel, use the back arrow or select anywhere outside the Printer panel.)

 Here's a handy keyboard shortcut that works in any app: Press ⊞+K to display the Devices panel. The shortcut Ctrl+P opens the Printer panel directly in some apps, but not all.

Figure 10-9

Edit Photos Using the Photos App

1. You can use the Photos app to change a photo, including making it smaller. In the Photos app, click one photo or tap for full-screen viewing.

2. Display the app bar (see Figure 10-6). The right side of the app bar offers tools for editing photos: Rotate, Crop, and Edit.

 Sometimes when you import photos from a digital camera, they arrive askew because the photographer turned the camera the wrong way when shooting. You can correct this error by selecting the Rotate button. Selecting this button turns the photo by 90 degrees. Keep selecting the button until the photo turns right-side-up.

3. Before you make any changes to this photo, consider saving a copy so you can retain the original. Making duplicates gives you some insurance against edits you can't undo, but you may not want to duplicate every photo.

4. Many photos can be improved by *cropping,* which involves cutting out distracting elements and keeping just part of the photo. You might crop a photo to concentrate on its most important part. To crop, select the Crop button. A box appears on the photo to indicate which parts will remain after cropping, as shown in **Figure 10-10**. To adjust the crop area, drag a corner of the box. As well, you can drag the photo itself to adjust the photo's placement.

 Selecting the right area can be awkward. To start over, select the Cancel button or press Esc.

Adjust the size of the box to determine what is cropped.

Figure 10-10

5. Select Apply. The selected area is all that remains, as shown in **Figure 10-11**. If you crop a very small area, you may want to zoom in to see the results.

 You can undo each step by selecting the Undo button.

6. If you want to save the changed photo, select the Update Original button.

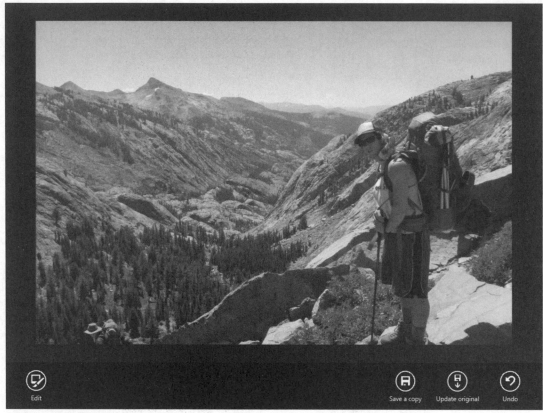

Edit

Save a copy   Update original   Undo

Figure 10-11

7. Select the Edit button to go to the Edit screen, as shown in **Figure 10-12**. On this screen, you can adjust the light and color of your photograph, as well as apply special effects. On a rainy day when you have nothing better to do, you can experiment with these tools. Select Light, for example, and you can adjust the brightness and contrast.

8. Using Auto Fix, you can take advantage of preset edits to photographs. Auto Fix presets appear on the right side of the screen. They offer the chance to change the light and color of a photograph in one fell swoop. Select the last preset, for example, to change your photo to black-and-white. Select Update Original if you want to save the edits you made to a photograph; press Esc or select Cancel if you decide not to keep your edits.

Choose an Auto Fix preset

Figure 10-12

 Windows Photo Gallery is a great tool for viewing, organizing, editing, and printing photos. Search the Store for the latest photo apps. See Chapter 12 for information on installing Windows Photo Gallery.

Enjoying Music and Videos

Chapter 11

*T*he term *media* on computers refers to something other than text: Audio and video are examples of media. *Audio* is a catchall term for music and other sound files, such as books on CD. *Video* includes files you can shoot with your digital camera, as well as Hollywood blockbusters.

The delivery of music has come a long way from Edison's wax cylinder or even vinyl LPs. Nowadays, music is entirely digital. The Music app lets you play your music collection and makes it easy to explore new music. Use Windows Media Player to play audio CDs and to copy audio files to your music library.

The Video app is similar to the Music app, but for video instead of music. You can use either app to buy new media, as well as play what you have.

In this chapter, you play a CD and copy CDs to the music folder for easier access. You also explore the Music and Video apps.

 You'll need a different app to play DVDs. Search Microsoft Store for Media Center or for a DVD player app. See Chapter 9 for more information on Microsoft Store.

Popular alternatives for music or videos include Amazon, Hulu, Netflix, and YouTube. All these are accessible through the web browser. Search Microsoft Store for related apps.

Play and Copy Music from a CD

1. If you have a CD or DVD disc drive or slot on your computer, insert a music CD, label side up for horizontal drives. (Vertical drives are less predictable.)

2. Windows 8.1 detects your CD and may briefly display a notification indicating *Tap to choose what happens with audio CDs.* (You can also click the notification.) If you're quick enough to tap or click the first notification, Windows 8.1 displays your choices, as shown in **Figure 11-1.** Select Windows Media Player, and then skip to Step 5.

Figure 11-1

 See Chapter 3 for information on increasing the time a notification remains on-screen.

3. If you missed the notification, go to the desktop and select the File Explorer icon (which looks like a folder) in the taskbar.

4. On the left side of File Explorer, select This PC, and then the drive below Local Disk C:. You may see the words *Audio CD*.

5. In the ribbon, select the Manage tab under Drive Tools. Then select AutoPlay. The notification from Step 1 reappears (and stays on-screen until you select something). Select Windows Media Player, unless the Music app is available, in which case select the Music app and skip to the next section.

6. If you see the Welcome to Windows Media Player screen, select Recommended Settings, and then select Finish. The Windows Media Player plays your music on the desktop. Switch back to the Start screen. The music continues to play. Switch back to the desktop.

7. For access to more options, select Switch to Library, a small button under the X in Windows Media Player, as shown in **Figure 11-2.**

Figure 11-2

8. Note the following controls at the bottom of the Media Player, as shown in **Figure 11-3**:

- **Shuffle:** Select this button to turn on *shuffle*, which randomly mixes the tracks you play. Select again to turn off shuffle, and the tracks play in the order in which they appear on-screen.

- **Repeat:** Select this button to play all the tracks again after all have played. Select again to turn off the repeat function.

- **Stop:** Select to stop playing.

- **Previous:** Select this button to skip to the previous track. Select and hold to rewind to an earlier point in the track.

- **Play/Pause:** Select the button with two vertical lines to pause play mid-track. Select the same button (now with a triangle pointing to the right) to resume playing from the point you paused.

- **Next:** Select this button to skip to the next track. Select and hold to fast-forward through the track.

- **Mute/Unmute:** Select this button to silence the player. Although the track continues to play, you won't hear it. When mute is on, a red circle with a slash appears next to the speaker icon. Select the button again to hear the track.

- **Volume:** Drag the slider to the left to decrease or to the right to increase the volume of the track. Your speakers may also have a manual volume control. Windows 8.1 has a separate volume control in the taskbar, as well.

- **Now Playing:** Located far to the right of the toolbar, select this button to reduce the player to a small size (refer to **Figure 11-2**).

Control music playback

Switch to Now Playing

Figure 11-3

9. To copy the CD tracks to your Music library, select Rip CD.

 Be sure to refer to this as *ripping a CD* around your younger friends. But not the youngest, because they think CDs are way passé and MP3s rule. (MP3 is an audio file format common to portable digital music players and music downloads.)

 If you're going to rip a lot of CDs, select Rip Settings⇨Rip CD Automatically and Rip Settings⇨Eject CD After Ripping. Just inserting the CD will copy files to your Music library as it plays the CD. Audiophiles should choose Rip Settings⇨Audio Quality⇨192 Kbps (Best Quality).

10. When the copying process finishes, remove your CD. To play this music in the future, start the Media Player and choose Artist, Album, or Genre under Music. You can also play anything in the Music library using the Music app. See the next section, "Listen to the Music App."

 Pin the Media Player to the taskbar for easy access: Click the right mouse button over the icon in the taskbar, or tap and hold until a box appears and then release. On the menu that pops up, select Pin This Program to Taskbar. You can also search for Windows Media Player on the Start screen. See Chapter 2 for information on pinning apps to the Start screen.

If your music CD doesn't play automatically the next time you insert one, you can tell Windows 8.1 how to handle audio CDs. On the Start screen, type **play CDs**. In the Search panel, select Play CDs or Other Media Automatically. The Control Panel opens to the AutoPlay settings. Scroll to the CDs section, and on the menu next to Audio CD, choose Play Audio CD (Windows Media Player). Then select Save. Switch back to the Start screen. Remove your CD, and then reinsert it. This method for changing AutoPlay may be helpful for other media types or devices.

Listen to the Music App

1. Select the Music app on the Start screen. The Xbox Music app home screen appears. If you see music here, ignore it for the moment. (Or select a song to play it, skip to Step 4, and do the rest of the steps some other time.) **Figure 11-4** shows the album I ripped from a CD in the preceding section. I can display this album by selecting it on the Collection screen.

Xbox Music

Search

Collection

Radio

Explore

⊕ New playlist

⊷ Import playlists

←

Le Chat Bleu [Expanded Edition]
Mink De Ville, 1980, Rock

▷ ⊕ ☰

1	This Must Be the Night	2:52
2	Savoir Faire	3:10
3	That World Outside	3:01
4	Slow Drain	3:30
5	You Just Keep Holding On	2:48
6	Lipstick Traces	2:49
7	Bad Boy	2:50
8	Mazurka	2:31

Figure 11-4

 If you see *Can't sign in*, you're not connected using a Microsoft account. You'll still be able to do the steps in this section. You need to sign in only to buy music.

2. To search for music by title or artist, type the text for which you want to look in the Search box. As you type, suggested matches appear below the Search box. For now, ignore these suggestions (but take advantage of them in the future to save typing). Instead, select the magnifying glass or press Enter. Search results appear on the left. Select any search result for the next step.

Selecting a suggested match may take you directly to Artist Details. Not a bad place to end up, but you can't easily get from there to the next step without repeating Step 2.

3. Scroll to the bottom of the Results screen to Songs and select a song. The album on which the song appears, and the song is selected, as shown in **Figure 11-5**. Note the following options (not all of which may appear on the current screen):

- **Play:** Connects your computer to Xbox Music and plays the song. Notice the controls at the bottom of the screen for pausing the song and controlling the volume (right-click the screen if you don't see these controls).

- **Play Album:** Plays the songs on the album, starting with song 1.

- **Add To:** Opens a pop-up menu with playlists you can add the song to.

- **Buy Album:** You must sign in to continue. An option to buy also appears if you select an individual song.

- **Explore Artist:** Opens a biographical page with information about the artist. Click the back arrow to return to the Results screen.

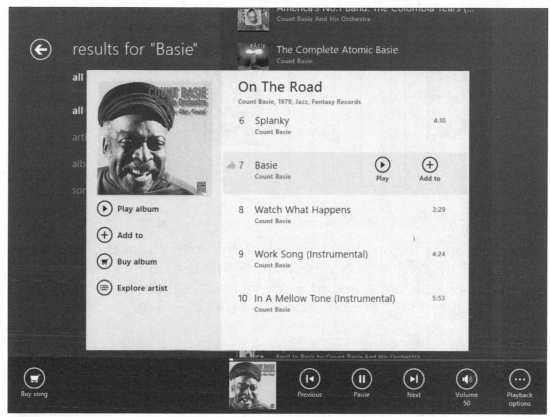

Figure 11-5

4. Check the volume level on your speakers. Tablets and laptops often have physical volume controls — look around the edges. To adjust volume levels using Windows 8.1, display the Settings panel. Select the speaker icon above the Power control, as shown in **Figure 11-6**. Slide the control up for more volume and down for less. Select the speaker icon to mute or unmute all sounds. Speakers should be unmuted but not so loud as to cause bleeding. Select anywhere in the Music app to dismiss the Settings panel.

Figure 11-6

5. Display the app bar, if necessary. Information for the currently playing song appears, including the album cover, song title, artist, and time played over total time (refer to **Figure 11-5**). Note the following controls:

- **Buy Song:** You are asked to sign in to your Microsoft account and confirm your purchase. You need an Xbox Music Pass to purchase songs.

- **Previous:** Go back one track.

- **Pause** or **Play:** Pause the track and the button changes to Play. Select Play to resume. There is no separate Stop button. You have to pause indefinitely or close the app.

- **Next:** Go forward one track.

- **Volume:** Drag the slider to control the volume.

- **Playback Options:** On the pop-up menu, choose Repeat to play the song again when it finishes playing; choose Shuffle to play album tracks randomly.

Your keyboard may have similar controls.

6. Switch back to the Start screen. The Music app continues to play. The Music tile displays the album art and title of the current song. Select the Music tile to return to the app.

 You may be able to play music from your computer to another device, such as another computer, a Windows Phone, an Xbox, or a TV on your network. Display the charms bar and select Devices to see if any are available.

7. Although you don't have to close the app, if you want to close the Music app or any other, use one of the following methods:

- **Mouse:** Move the mouse pointer to the top of the window. Click and drag down, and then release the mouse button.

- **Touchscreen:** Swipe down from the top edge until the app window shrinks. Lift your finger.

- **Keyboard:** Press Alt+F4.

Watch Videos

1. Select the Video app on the Start screen. The Xbox Video app home screen appears. See **Figure 11-7**. Scroll to the right for an overview of the Video home screen, noting Movies Store and TV Store. Scroll to the left, possibly past the first screen you saw, to see your videos, labeled *my videos*. If the Video library does not contain any videos, you may see *It's lonely here*. If you see videos here, ignore those videos for the moment.

Figure 11-7

 If you see *Can't sign in*, you're not connected using a Microsoft account. You'll be able to do the steps in this section. You need to be signed in only to buy or rent videos.

2. To search for videos by title or artist, click the Search icon in the upper-right corner of the screen. Then type the text for which you want to search. As you type, suggested matches appear below the text box. For now, ignore these suggestions (but take advantage of them in the future to save typing). Instead, select the magnifying glass or press Enter. Search results appear. Select any search result for the next step.

Selecting a suggested match may take you directly to the Details screen. Not a bad place to end up, but you can't easily get from there to the next step without repeating Step 3.

3. If the description screen opened, as shown in **Figure 11-8**, note the following options (not all of which may appear on the current screen):

Figure 11-8

- **View Seasons:** For a TV series, see information on the individual seasons and episodes.

- **Buy:** You must sign in to continue.

- **Rent:** You must sign in to continue.

- **Explore:** This option opens a biographical page with an overview of the movie or TV series.

- **Play Trailer:** Play the preview for the selected movie.

4. Select Play Trailer. (If you don't see that option, select a movie from the Video home screen or search for a movie.)

5. Check the volume level on your speakers. Tablets and laptops often have physical volume controls — look around the edges. To adjust volume levels using Windows 8.1, display the Settings panel. Select the speaker icon above the Power control (refer to **Figure 11-6**). Slide the control up for more volume and down for less volume. Select the speaker icon to mute or unmute all sounds. Speakers should be unmuted but not so loud as to cause bleeding. Select anywhere outside the Settings panel to dismiss it.

6. Display the app bar. Note the following controls, shown in **Figure 11-9**:

- **Get from Xbox 360:** Purchase this video for use on an Xbox 360 console.

- **Previous:** Go back.

- **Pause** or **Play:** Pause the video and the button changes to Play. Select Play to resume. There isn't a separate Stop button. You have to Pause indefinitely or close the app.

- **Next:** Go forward.

- **Volume:** Drag the slider to control the sound level.

- **Play on Xbox 360:** This option plays the selection on an Xbox game console.

Figure 11-9

 Your keyboard may have similar controls.

7. Switch back to the Start screen. The Video app pauses automatically — no need to use the Pause control. The Video tile displays the title of the video currently paused. Select the Video tile to return to the app, which automatically resumes playing.

 You may be able to play video from your computer to another device, such as another computer, a Windows Phone, an Xbox, or a TV on your network. Display the charms bar and select Devices to see if any are available.

8. Although you don't have to close the app, if you want to close the Video app or any other, use one of the following methods:

- **Mouse:** Move the mouse pointer to the top of the window. Click and drag down, and then release the mouse button.

- **Touchscreen:** Swipe down from the top edge until the app window shrinks, and then lift your finger.

- **Keyboard:** Press Alt+F4.

 For complete information on movies, TV, and the people involved in either, see www.imdb.com.

Part IV
Beyond the Basics

Update and recovery 🔍

Windows Update

File History

Recovery

Save copies of your files automatically

Automatically back up copies of your personal files on this PC in Documents,
Music, Pictures, Videos, and Desktop to a drive so you can get them back if
they're lost or damaged.

File History
Off ⬛

Back up your personal files on this PC to
My Passport (E:), 431 GB free of 465 GB

Select a different drive

Your files haven't been backed up.

Back up now

Visit www.dummies.com/extras/windows8dot1forseniors to find out
how to tell Windows 8.1 which app or program to use to open a file.

Maintaining Windows 8.1

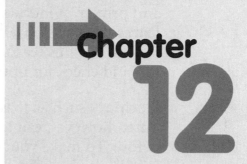

Chapter

12

*T*he desktop originated long before Windows
8.1. (In fact, desktops used to be made of
wood.) Now, the desktop has changed into
something more than just another app but less
than the Windows centerpiece it once was.

Windows 8.1 uses the *Action Center* to keep
you informed of security and maintenance
issues that may need attention, such as antivirus protection. The Action Center divides issues
into Security and Maintenance sections. The
Reliability Monitor can help you pinpoint
problems with hardware and software.

As millions of people put Windows 8.1 to the
test every single hour, Microsoft discovers
glitches with how Windows 8.1 works.
Especially important are weaknesses in security
that turn up only when software is under fire
in the real world. *Windows Update* is the process for installing *patches* (updates) to plug
these holes in Windows 8.1.

If you have an always-on Internet connection,
such as DSL or cable, Windows Update automatically downloads and installs the most
important updates as they become available
(usually, once a month). Security patches are
one of the most important updates, so they're
among the updates installed automatically.

Optional updates include updates to device *drivers*, the programs that make Windows 8.1 work with specific hardware, such as your display and printer. Windows Update keeps track of optional updates but leaves the decision of whether to install — and the installation — up to you. For this reason, you need to run Windows Update on the desktop and check for optional updates every few months.

Machines such as toaster ovens aren't getting any smarter. Your computer, however, can be programmed to do something it's never done before. To make your computer capable of doing new things, you install new programs. On the other hand, your computer may have some programs that you'll never use and wouldn't miss. You don't have to get rid of them, but doing so is easy enough and frees a little space on your computer.

In this chapter, you work with the Action Center and Windows Update. You also install a program on the desktop and, optionally, uninstall one.

 Updates to Windows 8.1 apps are handled by the Windows Store app on the Start screen. See Chapter 9 for information on updating individual apps.

Explore System Information on the Desktop

1. On the Start screen, select the Desktop tile. On the desktop, display the Settings panel using one of these techniques:

- **Mouse:** Move the mouse pointer into the lower-right corner of the screen. Select the Settings charm from the charms bar.

- **Touchscreen:** Swipe from the right edge and tap Settings.

- **Keyboard:** Press ⊞+I.

2. In the Settings panel, select PC Info. The System window in **Figure 12-1** appears. This screen is chock-full of information and functions. Note each of the following areas on screen:

- **Windows edition:** Of course, you have Windows 8.1. However, Windows 8.1 comes in two primary editions: the Standard edition, which you are likely to have, and the Pro edition, for computer professionals. You may find information here about so-called Service Packs, large collections of updates to Windows 8.1.

- **System:** This section displays details about your hardware, including the processor, the amount of installed memory (RAM), and other details.

System information on the desktop

Figure 12-1

- **Computer name, domain, and workgroup settings:** This information pertains to your network, if any. If a computer can't connect to a network, the problem is often related to the name of the Workgroup (a network). The Change Settings function lets you change the Workgroup name to match other computers on the same network. See Chapter 14 for information on networks, including homegroups.

- **Windows activation:** In an effort to control software piracy involving bootlegged copies of Windows 8.1, each copy of Windows 8.1 must be activated. Odds are that you activated your copy the first time you started your computer. If you don't see *Windows is activated* in this section, select the adjacent link.

 Don't be alarmed by the System information and options. If all goes well, you don't have to use most of what you find here. Some familiarity with this screen will be useful, however, is all doesn't go well later.

Check the Action Center

1. In the System window (refer to **Figure 12-1**), select Action Center in the lower-left corner. The Action Center window appears, as shown in **Figure 12-2**.

 Another way to open the Action Center is to search on the Start screen for **Action Center**, and then select Action Center in the search results.

Select these headings   Note any messages

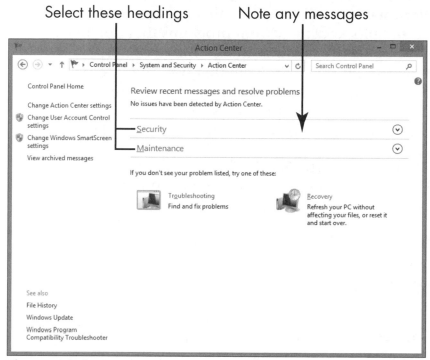

Figure 12-2

2. Note any message displayed under Review Recent Messages and Resolve Problems. Ideally, you see *No issues have been detected by Action Center.* If you see a message concerning a specific problem, select that message for more information.

3. Select the Security heading in the Action Center. That section expands to detail security functions. Every option but one should display *On* or *OK*. The exception is Network Access Protection, a function normally found in corporate environments. Here's a brief description of each item under Security:

- **Network Firewall:** The firewall scans Internet traffic and blocks activity from programs that don't have explicit permission to use Internet access. When you install a program that uses the Internet, you may be asked to approve the connection the first time. The safest practice is to reject online connections that you don't initiate or recognize.

- **Windows Update:** See the "Install Optional Updates" section for information on Windows Update.

- **Virus Protection:** Having virus protection for your computer is essential. Windows Defender provides antivirus protection, although you can install some other antivirus program.

- **Spyware and Unwanted Software Protection:** If this service is on, you have basic protection from malicious software provided by Windows Defender.

- **Internet Security Settings:** These settings pertain to your browser. The default settings may be adequate. To learn more, see the following tip.

 I recommend *Using the Internet Safely For Seniors For Dummies* by Nancy Muir and Linda Criddle (Wiley) as a guide for helping you deal with online security confidently.

- **User Account Control (UAC):** This function notifies you of programs that try to make changes to your system and requires that you confirm any such changes. In particular, UAC lets you know when a program tries to run or install software that may be malicious. When in doubt, say No or Cancel to UAC messages.

- **Windows SmartScreen:** This function blocks you from downloading programs, except through the Microsoft Store, as well as files capable of changing your system maliciously.

- **Network Access Protection (NAP):** If this service is off, that isn't a problem, unless the computer connects to a business network. NAP protects a business network from machines that aren't updated and secure.

- **Microsoft Account:** This one tells you whether your Microsoft account is set up properly.

4. Select the Maintenance heading to see what that section includes. Functions under Maintenance consist of the following:

- **Check for solutions to problem reports:** This setting is on, allowing Windows 8.1 to regularly check for solutions to problems it uncovers.

- **Automatic Maintenance:** Your computer automatically performs critical updates, security scans, and diagnostics each day.

 If your computer is in a guest room or bedroom, you may want to change the Automatic Maintenance setting to run maintenance tasks at some time other than the default 3:00 a.m. Your computer may actually wake up at that hour for maintenance, unless you use a power strip to turn off the computer after shutting down. If the computer can't run maintenance at the appointed hour, it will do so at the next opportunity.

- **HomeGroup:** A *homegroup* is a network that allows you to share files and printers between two or more computers. See Chapter 14 for information on networks, including homegroups.

- **File History:** See Chapter 15 for information on using the File History option, which is off by default.

- **Drive status:** *Drives* refers to hard disks inside or attached to your computer. Your documents, photos, and Windows 8.1 itself are stored on one or more drives. Ideally, the drive status is *All drives are working properly*. See Chapter 15 for information on backing up and restoring files.

 Action Center is a troubleshooting tool, so you should check it if you have problems running Windows 8.1.

5. Under Check for Solutions to Problem Reports, select View Reliability History. As shown in **Figure 12-3**, the Reliability Monitor screen graphs your computer's stability and indicates hardware and software problems, including those you may not be aware of. On this screen, red circles indicate critical events such as computer crashes; blue circles are information about software installation and updates; and yellow triangles indicate warnings about noncritical events (something that didn't crash the computer). Select a day in the graph to display details in the lower portion of the screen.

 Reviewing the Reliability Monitor screen will help you distinguish between a one-time glitch and a recurring or worsening problem.

 You can open the Reliability Monitor screen from the Start screen. Type **review reliability history** and then select View Reliability History in the search results.

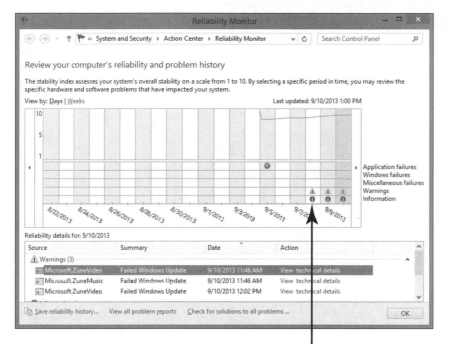

Select for more information

Figure 12-3

Install Optional Updates

1. In the System window (refer to **Figure 12-1**), select
   Windows Update in the lower-left corner. Windows
   Update appears on the desktop, as shown in **Figure** 12-4.
   (See Chapter 5 for information about working with the
   desktop.)

 Critical updates are installed automatically. Optional
   updates are just that — optional. Note, however, that
   optional updates may apply to computer hardware,
   such as your monitor or printer, and may improve
   performance or fix problems with devices.

Figure 12-4

2. In **Figure 12-4**, three optional updates are available. Your results may be different. Note the following information listed on the screen:

- **Most Recent Check for Updates:** The date and time when Windows 8.1 checked for updates, which should be the current day or very recent. If the most recent check is more than a week old, select the Check for Updates link on the left.

- **Updates Were Installed:** The date and time when Windows 8.1 was last updated. If you want to know what update was performed, select View Update History.

- **You Receive Updates:** Initially, Windows Update is *for Windows only.* See the section "Get Updates for Other Microsoft Programs," later in this chapter.

3. If you see a link indicating that you have optional updates available, select that link. The Select Updates to Install window appears, as shown in **Figure** 12-5. To learn more about an update, select its name. The area to the right then displays information for the selected update. Select the More Information link if you want to know even more.

 Note whether the update description includes a warning (marked by an exclamation point in a circle) that you may need to restart your computer after installing the update. In most cases, you won't have to restart immediately; you can shut down at the end of the day and start normally the next day.

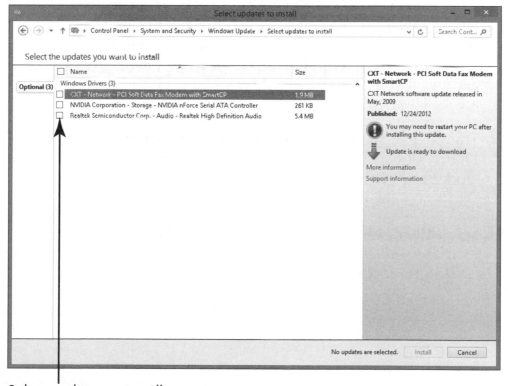

Select updates to install

Figure 12-5

4. Select the check box next to any or all updates you want to install. Then select the Install button. You can return to the Start screen and do other things during installation, but don't close this window or shut down your computer until the screen indicates installation is complete.

Get Updates for Other Microsoft Programs

1. If you use Microsoft software other than Windows — in particular, Word (for word processing) or Excel (spreadsheet app) — you can have Windows Update check for updates to those programs, as well. (Your Microsoft programs are already being updated if the Windows Update screen says that you receive updates *for Windows and other products from Microsoft Update.* Skip to Step 3 to update your Microsoft programs). In the desktop Windows Update screen (refer to **Figure 12-4**), select Change Settings if you need to change how Microsoft programs are updated on your computer.

2. The Change Settings window opens, as shown in **Figure 12-6**. Select the check box next to Give Me Updates for Other Microsoft Products When I Update Windows. Then select OK.

3. Select Check for Updates to update your Microsoft programs as well as Windows. Windows Update automatically starts and searches for updates.

Figure 12-6

Install a New Program on the Desktop

1. You can install software that you download from the Web or from a CD or DVD for use on the desktop. (Windows 8.1 apps must be installed through the Microsoft Store.) In this set of steps, you install Windows Photo Gallery, my favorite free program for editing photos. To install Photo Gallery, first switch to the desktop. Select the blue *e* in the taskbar to run Microsoft Internet Explorer (MSIE). Enter **get.live.com** in the address bar. (See Chapter 6 for information on using Microsoft Internet Explorer.)

If a website offers to install a program automatically, look at that suggestion with suspicion. It may be legitimate or it may be malevolent. Decline downloads from sources that you don't know and trust already.

2. On the Windows Essentials web page, select the Learn More link under Photo Gallery. On the Photo Gallery page, select Download Now.

3. Internet Explorer displays a message at the bottom of the browser window, as shown in **Figure 12-7**. Select the Run button. If the User Account Control dialog box appears, select the Yes button to indicate that you want to download and install the program.

4. Note that Internet Explorer displays a progress indicator at the bottom of the browser window. When the download is complete, Internet Explorer performs a security scan of the program. Then, the User Account Control asks for confirmation to continue with the installation. Select the Yes button.

5. The Windows Essentials screen appears. Select Choose the Programs You Want to Install. On the Select Programs to Install screen, deselect everything except Photo Gallery and Movie Maker (one option). Then, select Install.

Generally, if the installer for a program offers Express or Custom installation options, choose the Express option to let the installer set up the program without further input from you. The Custom or Advanced Settings option allows you to specify where to install the program and, perhaps, which parts of the program to install.

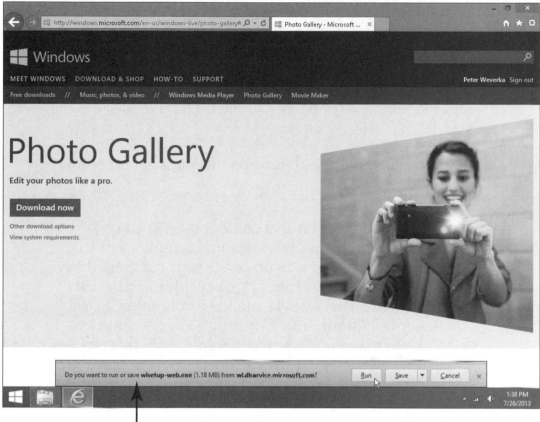

Internet Explorer message

Figure 12-7

6. A moving bar indicates the progress of the installation, which should take a few minutes. On the screen that indicates installation is done, select the Close button.

 Many programs try to connect to the Internet for updates during installation or when you run the installed program. The first time you run a program, you may be asked if you want to register the program or configure some aspect of the program. Go with the default (assumed) responses, if you're not sure.

7. To run Photo Gallery, switch to the Start screen, type **photo gallery**, and select the Photo Gallery tile in the search results. Photo Gallery opens on the desktop. If you see the Sign In with Your Email Address screen, enter your Microsoft account e-mail address and password, select Remember My ID and Password, and then select Sign In. (Or select Cancel.)

8. Photo Gallery, like the Photo app, displays photos from your Photo Library.

 To install a program that comes on a CD or DVD, insert the program disc into your computer's disc drive or tray, label side up (or, if your computer has a vertical disc slot, insert the disc with the label side facing left). The AutoPlay dialog box appears. Select the option to run Install or Setup. User Account Control may ask if you really want to run this program. (Windows 8.1 tries to keep you from installing software unintentionally by asking for confirmation.)

Remove Desktop Programs

1. Unlike Windows 8.1 apps from the Microsoft Store, desktop programs are installed and uninstalled directly through the desktop itself. To see which desktop programs are installed, select Control Panel Home on the System, Action Center, or Windows Update screen. See the first section in this chapter, "Explore System Information on the Desktop," for steps.

 Most of the functions covered in this chapter are part of Control Panel, which presents many functions for tweaking your computer setup. You can also access Control Panel through the Settings charm while on the desktop.

2. In the Control Panel window (shown in **Figure** 12-8), under Programs, select Uninstall a Program. (You don't have to uninstall anything; you can simply see what the option offers.)

Uninstall a program or just look
Figure 12-8

3. The Programs and Features window lists desktop programs, not Windows 8.1 apps. Initially, these programs are sorted by name. You may want to see the date you last used each program because a program you haven't used in ages may be a safe one to remove. (Otherwise, skip to Step 5.) Use one of the following techniques to display the date last used:

   • **Mouse:** Move the mouse pointer over any column heading, such as Name. Click the right mouse button.

- **Touchscreen:** Tap and hold down on any column heading, such as Name. When a box appears around your fingertip, lift your finger.

4. On the context menu that appears, select More. In the Choose Details window (shown in **Figure 12-9**), select Last Used On, and then select the OK button. The Last Used On column appears to the right of all the other columns.

 Unfortunately, Last Used On may be blank. In fact, even if you just used Photo Gallery in the previous section, nothing appears in the Last Used On column.

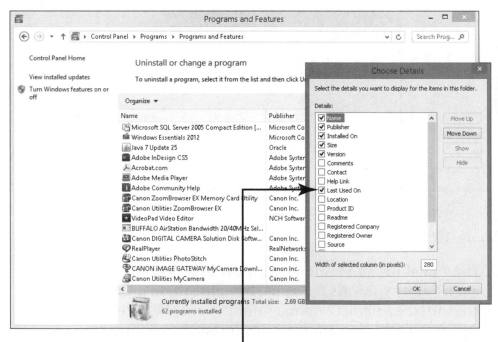

Select the Last Used On option

Figure 12-9

5. To change a program, select it. For this example, select Windows Essentials, as shown in **Figure 12-10**. You don't have to uninstall Photo Gallery, but if you do, you can follow the steps in the preceding section to reinstall it.

Select to uninstall

Figure 12-10

6. Select the Uninstall/Change button. The Windows Essentials screen offers options to Remove One or More or to Repair All. Some programs will offer an option to Change the program as well. Repair or Change may be useful for a desktop program that you want to keep but that isn't running as expected. Select Remove One or More Windows Essential Programs or Cancel. If you selected Remove, select Photo Gallery and Movie Maker on the next screen, then select Uninstall. (Your photos are not removed.)

7. If you uninstalled Photo Gallery or another program, it will no longer appear in the Programs and Features window or on the Start screen.

 Just because you can uninstall a program doesn't mean you should. You can simply ignore programs you don't use. Look at a program's name, publisher, and date installed to determine whether you actually use a program. You may recognize a program you installed recently, as opposed to one installed before you got your computer. If you find that it's more productive to remove large programs than small ones, repeat Steps 3 and 4 to group by size.

 Before you uninstall a program that you may want to reinstall later, make sure that you have a copy of it on a CD or DVD (or that you know where to download it from the Web again). You have no undo option when you uninstall a program.

Connecting a Printer and Other Devices

Chapter 13

Every computer has a screen. Most computers, other than tablets, also have a keyboard and a mouse or other pointing device. You can add a mouse to a laptop that lacks one or replace the keyboard or mouse that came with your computer. Add a printer or a scanner to extend your computer's functionality.

For any hardware add-ons — which tech-folk call *peripherals* — Windows 8.1 has a trick up its sleeve. Thanks to *plug and play* technology, which automatically identifies add-on devices, connecting new devices to your computer can be quite easy.

In this chapter, you explore the devices connected to your computer, as well as options available for those devices. You find out how to access devices connected to your computer and also calibrate a touchscreen to make it work better for you.

Trust USB Plug and Play for Hardware

You may find many kinds of add-on devices useful:

➡ A **printer** lets you, well, print documents and photos. Your choices for printers include black and white versus color, and inkjet versus laser printer. Multifunction printers also work as a copier, scanner, and fax machine.

➡ A **digital camera** captures photos that you can copy to your computer to enjoy and to share with others. See Chapter 10 for information on working with photos.

➡ A **scanner** enables you to make digital images of old photos or documents so that you can view them on-screen.

➡ An **external hard drive** stores backup copies of your files. See Chapter 15 for information on adding a hard drive to your computer.

➡ An additional or replacement **pointing device** (your mouse is a pointing device), including a trackball or a pen with a tablet, may be more comfortable to use than what came with your computer. Switching between pointing devices helps you avoid repetitive stress. A wireless mouse eliminates the hassle of dealing with a cord. Some people like to add a mouse as an alternative to their laptop's built-in touchpad.

➡ A **microphone** is crucial for communicating by voice with your computer, through speech recognition, or with your friends over the Internet. A combination headset with microphone may produce the clearest sound.

➡ A **video camera** (or *webcam*) is essential for video phone calls *a la* the Jetsons. See Chapter 10 for information on using a webcam.

The majority of these devices connect using *USB* (Universal Serial Bus) technology. When you connect a device to your computer using a USB cable to the USB port (see **Figure 13-1**), the device identifies itself to the computer. This identification process is called *plug and play.* Ideally, you connect your device, and it simply works.

Windows 8.1 uses a *device driver* to communicate with an add-on device. The driver is really a program that tells Windows 8.1 how to run the device. When you connect a device, such as a printer, Windows 8.1 looks for a driver (in this case, a *printer driver*). That driver may be built into Windows 8.1, come on a disc that's packaged with the device, or need to be downloaded from the Internet, either automatically by Windows 8.1 or manually by you.

USB port   USB cable

Figure 13-1

Every computer has at least a couple of USB ports. Some are in the front, and others are in the back of the computer and harder to reach. If your computer doesn't have enough ports, you can add more by buying a USB hub, which is a small box with two to four USB ports. If a port is hard to reach with a device's cable, you can buy a USB extension cable. Office supply stores may have hubs and cables.

 Bluetooth is a wireless technology for adding devices to your computer. If your computer has Bluetooth, you can use Bluetooth as well as USB to add some devices, especially a microphone or headset.

See All Devices

1. On the Start screen, type **devices**. Select Device Settings in the Search panel. The Devices category of the PC and Devices window appears, as shown in **Figure 13-2**.

 To search using a touchscreen, swipe from the right edge to display the charms bar. Select the Search charm. Then select in the search box to display the virtual keyboard.

2. Note the specific devices that appear on the right, and scroll down the screen to see all your devices. Devices listed may include your monitor, speakers, headphones, keyboard, mouse, and more. Devices shared through your homegroup or network also appear here. For information on adjusting device settings, see the "Access Device Options on the Desktop" section, later in the chapter.

(←) PC and devices   🔍

Lock screen

Display

Devices

Mouse and touchpad

Typing

Corners and edges

Power and sleep

AutoPlay

PC info

Add devices

[+] Add a device

Printers

🖨 Canon Inkjet MX700 series (Copy 1) on OWNER-PC

🖨 Canon Inkjet MX700 series on OWNER-PC
     Offline

🖨 Microsoft XPS Document Writer

🖨 Quicken PDF Printer

Other devices

📶 BUFFALO WLI-UC-GNM Wireless LAN Adapter

🖥 DELL IN1910N

📶 LANDevice

🔊 Line In (High Definition Audio Device)

List of printers, screens, and more

Figure 13-2

 Some, but not all, devices display information below the device name. A network device may display *Offline* (not accessible) or may display nothing if it is accessible. A printer may display *Ready* or may display nothing if the printer isn't ready.

 You are unlikely to need the Add a Device button because most devices are added *automagically* (that's a word nerds like to use). However, if you select Add a Device, Windows 8.1 scans for additional hardware. No harm in doing so.

Connect a Printer or Other Device

1. Take your printer out of the box. Keep all the packing material together until you know you won't need to return the printer. Arrange all the components for easy access. In addition to the printer, you'll probably find ink cartridges or a toner cartridge, a power cable, and a CD with printer software. Read the setup instructions that come with your printer.

 Some of these steps apply to other devices, such as a mouse, a webcam, or a microphone. Printers often have more packaging and require more assembly than other devices.

2. Remove all tape from the printer. Most printers ship with the print mechanism locked in place to prevent it from moving during shipping. Look for brightly colored tape, paper, or plastic indicating what you need to move or remove to release the print mechanism.

3. Put the printer within cable length of your computer. Insert the ink or toner cartridge before you turn on the printer for the first time. Place some paper in the paper drawer or tray. Connect the printer to the power supply. Plug the printer cable into the printer and into the computer.

 Your printer may have come with a disc with a printer driver and other software. You don't need that disc unless Windows 8.1 fails to correctly install a driver automatically.

4. Turn on the printer. You may see some informational messages as Windows 8.1 handles the configuration.

5. To confirm that your printer is installed properly, see the preceding section, "See All Devices."

Access Device Options on the Desktop

1. For more control over device setup, search for **devices and printers** on the Start screen. Then select Devices and Printers to display the window shown in **Figure 13-3**.

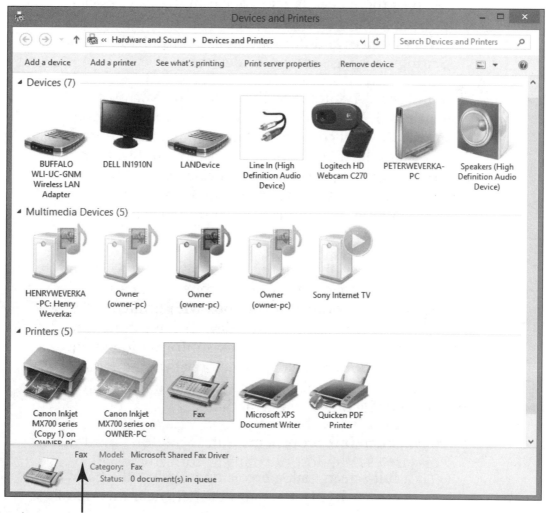

Select a device to access options

Figure 13-3

2. The Device and Printers window shows the devices attached to your computer, including the computer itself, the display (or monitor), external add-on devices (such as a hard drive, flash drive, or memory card), and the mouse.

 Most of these devices also appear in the Devices category of PC and Devices. However, you'll find options under Devices and Printer that aren't available in PC Settings, such as settings for devices.

 Windows 8.1 automatically installs the Microsoft XPS Document Writer. This device doesn't print but does create files you could print later using a real printer. For example, if you're in a coffee shop and want to print a web page or an e-mail message, you could use this device and then open the file it creates when your computer is connected to a printer. (That file will open in Reader.)

3. Double-click or double-tap the device you want to examine. This action opens the device's properties in a window with options or in a smaller box with limited information and options. (Older devices have more limited information.) **Figure 13-4** shows information about a fax machine. When you're finished reviewing the information or selecting available options, return to the previous screen using one of these methods:

- If a small box is open, close it.

- If a full-screen dialog box is open, select the back arrow or select Devices and Printers near the top of the window.

Canon MX700 series FAX

« Devices and Printers ▸ Canon MX700 series FAX   Search Can... 🔍

Canon MX700 series FAX

Inkjet Multifunction Printer

📄 0 document(s) in ...   🖨 Letter,Portrait   **Canon**

Printer Management
Operate your printer
Display Print Queue | Display Printer Properties

Scanner Management
Operate your scanner
Scan Photos or Documents | Display Scan Profiles for WIA Driver

Storage Medium Management
Operate the files saved on the storage medium
Copy Images | Browse Files

Support
Support & Service
Windows OS Support | USA

Some devices offer several options

Figure 13-4

4. Display the context menu of options for your printer (or
any device) using one of these methods (use the XPS
device if you don't have another printer): Click the right
mouse button or tap and hold until you see a small box
appear under your finger and then release. Select Printer
Properties from the menu. (Oddly, the menu also has a
separate Properties option — be sure to select Printer
Properties, instead.)

5. In the Properties window, select the Print Test Page button. Another window opens indicating *A test page has
been sent to your printer*. Select Close.

 If a test page doesn't print, check that both ends of
the cable are plugged in properly and make sure the
printer is turned on. Try to print a test page again.
For more help, contact the printer manufacturer or
the store where you bought the printer, or search
the Web.

If you're having problems with any device, select the Troubleshoot option on the context menu to open a guided troubleshooting program that will walk you through options for resolving problems with the device.

 The top of the Devices and Printers window has the Add a Device and Add a Printer button, but you need to use them only if Windows 8.1 doesn't automatically detect and install your device. With USB and plug and play, most devices install automatically.

Calibrate Your Touchscreen

1. If you have a problem accurately selecting objects on your screen using touch, you can calibrate your screen alignment. On the Start screen, type **touch**. Then select Calibrate the Screen for Pen or Touch Input.

2. In the Tablet PC Settings window, select the Calibrate button, as shown in **Figure 13-5**. User Account Control may ask you to confirm that you want to run the Digitizer Calibration Tool. If so, select Yes.

 If your touchscreen is badly calibrated, you may not be able to tap the Calibrate button. In that case, plug in a mouse to make the selection, and then continue using touch.

 Ignore the option to Choose the Order in Which Your Screen Rotates. Windows 8.1 tablets automatically rotate the screen content as you turn the tablet. Look for the orientation lock on your tablet. If orientation lock is on, the screen will not rotate between portrait (vertical) and landscape (horizontal).

Tablet PC Settings

Display | Other

Configure

Configure your pen and touch displays.

[Setup...]

Display options

Display: 1. Acer T231H ▾

Details: Touch Input Available

[Calibrate...] [Reset...]

Choose the order in which your screen rotates.
Go to Orientation

[OK] [Cancel] [Apply]

Figure 13-5

3. The screen displays lines around its perimeter, forming a box near the edge of the screen and a second box inside the first about half an inch from the edge. Lines connect these boxes near each corner. The result is 16 intersections. Starting at the upper-left corner, use your finger or a stylus to tap each intersection, which displays two short black lines forming crosshairs. As you touch each intersection, Windows 8.1 adjusts settings according to your touch. If that touch is accepted, the crosshairs move to the next intersection to the right. If not, tap the previous intersection again. As the crosshairs move, tap the highlighted intersection, left to right, down, then left to right again. The process takes much longer to read about than to do.

 If Windows 8.1 doesn't recognize your touch, it won't continue with the process. The screen says *Right-click anywhere to return to the last calibration point.* What if you don't have a mouse? Tap and hold until you see the little box under your fingertip, and then release — that's the touch equivalent of a click of the right mouse button.

4. After you have selected each of the 16 calibration points in turn, a box pops up asking whether or not you want to save the calibration data. Select OK unless you think something went wrong. In that case, select Cancel.

 It's unlikely but possible that you can't continue to the end of the process. If so, the screen says *Press the Esc button to close the tool.* What if you don't have a keyboard? In that case, press and hold the Windows button (with the four-part Windows logo) on the tablet edge as you also press the power button, and then release both. On the next screen, select Task Manager. In the Task Manager window, select Digitizer Calibration Tool, and then select the End Task button. Makes one yearn for an Esc.

Organizing Your Documents

Chapter 14

*E*verything inside your computer is stored on a disk. Your computer has a primary disk, formally called the internal *hard drive*. You may see this disk referred to as the C: drive. (The terms *drive* and *disk* are interchangeable.)

The contents of a disk are organized into individual files. When you save a document, you create a file on a disk. Many other files on the disk belong to the programs you use, including the thousands of files that make up Windows 8.1.

Disks also are organized into *folders*, which are containers for files. For its own files, Windows 8.1 has a main folder that contains dozens of other folders (called *subfolders*). Inside or below that user account folder, Windows 8.1 creates more folders to help you organize your files by type. For example, by default all your photos go into the Pictures folder, and all your documents go into the Documents folder.

In this chapter, you search for files and explore your disk, folders, and documents. You work with File Explorer as you create new folders to organize documents and move files from one folder to another. You also copy files from your hard disk to other disks to take with you or give to other people. File management is much more exciting than it may sound so far.

Find a Misplaced File

1. To search for a misplaced file, begin on the Start screen. Type the name of a document or photo you have on your computer. The search results panel appears, as shown in Figure 14-1.

Search

Everywhere ∨

sierra

Sierra - group

Sierra - moonrise

sierra central credit union

sierra trading post

sierra vista herald

sierra college

sierra bullets

sierra club

Figure 14-1

 To search using a touchscreen, swipe from the right edge to display the charms bar. Select the Search charm. Select in the search box to display the virtual keyboard.

 The keyboard shortcut for Search is ⊞+Q (for query).

2. Initially, the search panel shows settings, files, web images, and web videos in the search results. If you don't see the document or photo you want, narrow the list of items by opening the Everywhere drop-down menu and choosing Files, as shown in **Figure 14-2**.

Select Files to narrow your search to files

Figure 14-2

3. To open a file found in Step 1 or 2, select that file. Then, close the app that opens that file by using one of these methods:

- **Mouse:** Move the mouse pointer to the top of the screen. When the pointer changes to a hand symbol, click and hold down the left mouse button. Drag the app down until part of the app is off the bottom of the screen. Then release the left mouse button to close the app and return to the Start screen.

- **Touchscreen:** Swipe down from the top of the screen until part of the app is off the bottom of the screen. Then lift your finger to close the app and return to the Start screen.

- **Keyboard:** Press Alt+F4.

Strictly speaking, if you find what you're looking for, stop looking. (No extra charge for pearls of wisdom.) In this case, however, keep looking because doing so reveals important information about how files are organized and how you can take control of that organization.

4. On the Start screen, select the Desktop tile. On the desktop, select the File Explorer icon (the yellow folder) in the taskbar. File Explorer opens. Note the *ribbon*, which is the collapsible toolbar at the top of the window, as shown in **Figure 14-3**.

Collapse or expand the ribbon

Figure 14-3

 On the ribbon, tools are grouped by tabs, which in File Explorer consist of File, Home, Share, and View, as well as other tabs that appear based on the selection. Tabs are further divided into sections, labeled below the related tools. (Note, for example, the Clipboard section on the Home tab.) To expand the ribbon, select the up arrow at the far right of the tabs. Collapse the ribbon by selecting the down arrow.

Select a tab to display its tools, whether the ribbon is expanded or collapsed.

5. Select the box labeled *Search* (probably followed by *This PC*), below the ribbon and to the right. Type the same search term you used in Step 1. As you type, File Explorer displays any matching files, highlighting the text that matches. **Figure** 14-4 shows the results of a search on my computer using the search term *sierra*.

Type your search term

Figure 14-4

On a touchscreen, the virtual keyboard doesn't appear on the desktop until you select the keyboard icon on the right side of the taskbar.

If the search results include too many files, making it hard to see the one you want, type more of the file name in the Search box. The number of matching files should decrease as you type more text in the box.

6. The *focus* of a search — where File Explorer searches —
determines what files and folders are found. Because File
Explorer opens with the focus on This PC, your initial
search looks for files and folders throughout your computer. To change the focus on your search to the Pictures
folder, select the Pictures folder in the Navigation pane,
as shown in **Figure 14-5.** Then select the box labeled
Search, select the Current Folder button, and enter your
search term again. The search results focus on files in the
Pictures folder.

You can use Search Tools in the ribbon to refine a
search, as needed. Start a search, and then select the
Search tab. In the section labeled Refine, select Date
Modified and then select a time period ranging from
Today to Last Year. Select Kind to limit the search to
specific types of files. You can even select by size and
other properties.

Select a folder

Choose Current Folder to change the focus

Figure 14-5

Use File Explorer for Easy Access to Files

1. On the desktop, select the File Explorer icon in the task-bar. The right side of Explorer is called the *content area*. The left side of Explorer is called the *navigation pane* and contains folders. Explorer starts with its focus on your Favorites and This PC folders, and on your C drive and Network drives (if your computer is connected to a network).

 The keyboard shortcut to open File Explorer is ⊞+E. You don't need to switch to the desktop before using the shortcut.

2. On the left, select Music, then Pictures, and then Videos, while noting the files in the content area on the right. Many Windows 8.1 apps store files by default in the Documents, Music, Pictures, and Videos folders. Select the Documents folder again.

3. To create a practice document you can use in later sections, select the Home tab in the ribbon. In the New section, select New Item, and then select Text Document, as shown in **Figure 14-6**. (If you don't see this option, make sure that the Documents folder is selected.) An empty text document is created and the words *New Text Document* are highlighted so you can type a new name. Type **practice file**. (You'll rename this file in a later section.) Feel free to repeat this step to create additional items for practice, including Microsoft Word Documents or Bitmap Images.

Select New Item to create an empty document

Figure 14-6

 On a touchscreen, the virtual keyboard doesn't appear on the desktop until you select the keyboard icon on the right side of the taskbar.

4. Select the View tab in the ribbon. In the Layout section, select each option, such as Extra Large Icons and Large, Medium, and Small Icons. If you see a downward-pointing triangle on the right edge of the Layout options, select that triangle to display even more options. Try them all, if you like.

 Certain layouts are better for certain purposes. For example, photos are easier to recognize as Extra Large Icons than as a List. **Figure 14-7** shows my documents using the Details view, which includes the date the file was modified.

Details view shows the file modification date

Figure 14-7

 The more time you spend in File Explorer, the more worthwhile it is to explore the ribbon as you need it.

Create or Join a Homegroup

1. On the Start screen, type **homegroup**. On the search results screen, select Choose HomeGroup and Sharing Options. This opens the HomeGroup category of PC Settings.

 On a touchscreen, the virtual keyboard doesn't appear on the desktop until you select the keyboard icon on the right side of the taskbar.

A *homegroup* is a simple *network*, which is a connection between two or more computers for the purpose of sharing resources, such as an Internet connection, files, printers, and storage. One user on a network creates a homegroup that other users join, if they choose.

You can also create or join a homegroup by selecting Homegroup in the navigation pane of File Explorer.

2. If *A Homegroup Is Available* appears on screen, select the Enter the Homegroup Password box. Type the password and select Join.

 The person who created the homegroup can give you the password. If that person doesn't remember it, he or she can follow the steps in this section on his or her own machine to get the password for you.

 If you see *HomeGroup Is Only Available on a Home Network*, jump to the "Browse for a Network" section, later in this chapter.

 If you are the first person to use this function in your household or you have already joined a homegroup, the right side of the screen displays the settings for choosing what to share with the homegroup.

3. For each folder and device that you want to share, click or tap to the right of the small black box in the rectangular slider, as shown in **Figure 14-8**.

 Folders and devices shared in the homegroup will appear in the file picker and other places where you save or open files, including File Explorer.

 If you want to turn off sharing for a folder or device, click or tap to the left of the black box that appears in the rectangular slider.

4. Scroll down, if necessary, to see the Password section. The password required by other users to join your homegroup appears in the box.

Click or tap to the right to share

Figure 14-8

 Although you can change this password through a long series of steps, you'll use this password only when a computer joins a homegroup for the first time.

 In the unlikely event that you want to leave a homegroup, select the Leave button at the bottom of the HomeGroup screen. I don't recommend this because doing so removes all options for sharing through HomeGroup.

5. Switch to the desktop and open File Explorer. On the left, select Homegroup. If you have created or joined a homegroup, you'll see your computer and others that have joined. By selecting objects in the homegroup, you can access anything shared by others.

Browse for a Network

1. On the Start screen, type **network**. On the search results screen, select the Network app. The Network window opens on the desktop.

 To search using a touchscreen, swipe from the right edge to display the charms bar. Select the Search charm. Then select in the search box to display the virtual keyboard.

2. In the Network window, you may see icons for other computers on your network, as well as your own. My network is shown in **Figure 14-9**. Your screen may show only two or three computers. Select one of the other computers. Shared resources will appear in the window. (You may be asked for a user name and password, obtainable from the user of that computer.)

 The difference between a homegroup and a network is subtle. A homegroup is specific kind of network and may be easier to create than a network. A network has more options and can give you finer control over access to sharing. Take the easy route: Use an existing homegroup or network or create a homegroup.

Select Network

Figure 14-9

3. If you see the message *Network discovery and file sharing are turned off. Network computers and devices are not visible. Click to change…* just below the ribbon, select that message. Then select Turn On Network Discovery and File Sharing on the pop-up menu. This option enables your computer to find other computers and to be found by others.

If you're on a public network, don't turn on network discovery.

4. Select the Network tab, and then select Network and Sharing Center. If *Access type* indicates *No network access*, select Troubleshoot Problems. On the Troubleshoot Problems screen, select Internet Connections. On the next screen, select Troubleshoot My Connection to the Internet. This troubleshooter runs through a series of diagnostics to resolve the problem. After a few minutes, the screen will display *Troubleshooting has completed.* You may then see *Problems found,* as well as an indication of whether those problems have been fixed.

 At this point, if you still have a problem accessing the network or resources on the network, restart your computer. See Chapter 4 for information on connecting to the Internet. See Chapter 12 for information on maintaining Windows 8.1.

Create a Folder to Organize Your Files

1. In the File Explorer navigation pane, select the Documents folder.

2. On the Home tab, select the New Folder button. An icon for the new folder appears in the content area on the right, with the name *New folder* next to it and already selected (see **Figure 14-10**).

Select the New Folder button

Figure 14-10

On a touchscreen, the virtual keyboard doesn't appear on the desktop until you select the keyboard icon on the right side of the taskbar.

3. Type **practice folder** as the new name. Don't move the cursor or mouse before you start typing. Your new text will replace the highlighted text automatically. Press the Enter key to make the new name stick. (If you have a problem naming the folder, see the "Rename a File or a Folder" section, later in this chapter.)

4. Open your new folder by double-clicking or double-tapping its icon. The content area is empty.

5. To return to the Documents folder, select Documents in the navigation pane.

 Don't worry too much about creating folders, because the folders Windows 8.1 provides may be all you ever need. As you accumulate more files, however, placing them into other folders may help you stay organized. In the Documents folder, for example, you might create a subfolder called Finances for files related to income, expenses, and investments, and another subfolder called Family for family-related documents. Which folders and subfolders to create and how to name them depends entirely on your own sense of order.

Add a Location to Favorites

1. If you frequently access a specific location using File Explorer, you can add that location to the Favorites section of the navigation pane for easy access. For this exercise, select the Documents folder. (These steps work for folders, not files.)

2. Select the folder you created in the preceding section (or any other folder).

3. On the Home tab, select the Easy Access button. From the drop-down list, select Add to Favorites (see **Figure 14-11**). A *shortcut* to your selected location appears at the bottom of the Favorites section in the navigation pane.

Select the Easy Access button

Figure 14-11

 To remove a shortcut from Favorites, select the Favorites heading, and then select the item you want to remove. Select the Delete button on the Home tab. This action deletes just the shortcut, not the original folder.

 The Easy Access button also has an option to Pin to Start, which adds a tile for this location to the Start screen.

Use Check Boxes to Select Files

1. In File Explorer, you select files to move, copy, rename, or delete. You can add a check box to make selecting multiple files easier. In Explorer, select the View tab, and then select the Options button. The Folder Options window appears. Select the View tab (in the Folder Options window, not in the Explorer ribbon), as shown in **Figure 14-12**. Scroll through the Advanced Settings box until you see Use Check Boxes to Select Items, and then select that check box. Select the OK button.

Select this option

Figure 14-12

2. Select the Documents folder (or any folder that contains more than one file). To select a file, click or tap the area to the left of the file name. (You won't see the check box until you select it with a tap or a click or hover over it with the mouse pointer.) Repeat to select additional files. If you want to deselect a file, select the check box again to remove the check mark. Close the window after you've seen how these check boxes work. **Figure 14-13** shows four selected files.

Select a file by using its check box

Figure 14-13

 If you want to select only a single file, you can select anywhere on the file name. You use the check box when you want to select more than one file at a time.

 The Home tab has other methods for selecting. Select All does just what it says — selects all objects in a folder or library. Select None works similarly. Invert Selection switches the selection. For example, if I chose Invert Selection in the context of **Figure 14-13,** the four selected files would be deselected and all the other files would be selected. Sometimes it's easier to select the files you don't want and then invert the selection.

Add the Undo Button to File Explorer

1. You can add a button to File Explorer to undo an action, such as moving, renaming, or deleting a file. Above the Home tab, select the rather small down-pointing arrow to display the Customize Quick Access Toolbar list, as shown in **Figure 14-14**.

Figure 14-14

2. Select the Undo option from the drop-down list. The Undo button, which sports a blue arrow curving to the left, appears immediately to the left of the arrow you clicked in Step 1. You can undo most — but not all — actions in File Explorer by clicking or tapping this button immediately after the action. (Time isn't the issue. You can do something, and then undo it a year later if you don't do anything in the meantime.)

 The keyboard shortcut for undo is Ctrl+Z. This shortcut works regardless of whether the Undo button is on the screen.

 You may be able to undo a series of actions by repeating the undo function.

3. Select the Customize Quick Access Toolbar button again. Note that you can also add the Redo button, which, as you would expect, undoes the undo. All the other options appear also on larger buttons on the Home tab, so you don't need to add them to the Quick Access toolbar.

Move a File from One Folder to Another

1. You can move files to organize them. For this exercise, select the Documents folder in File Explorer. Select one of your documents.

 To move more than one file at a time, see the section "Use Check Boxes to Select Files."

2. On the Home tab, select the Move To button, as shown in **Figure 14-15**.

Select the Move To button

Figure 14-15

3. If you see the location you want in the drop-down list, you could select that location. However, for practice, select Choose Location. A window opens, showing every possible location, as shown in **Figure 14-16**. Select Documents, and then the practice folder you created in the section "Create a Folder to Organize Your Files." (Or select the Make New Folder button and name that folder.) Finally, select the Move button.

Select a location

Figure 14-16

 Unless you move many files or large files, you may not see any indication that the move was completed.

4. In Explorer, select the folder to which you moved your file. There it is!

 Note that the Copy To button works similarly, except the original file stays where it is and a copy is created in the new location.

Use these same steps to move a subfolder from one folder to another. However, don't move folders that Windows 8.1 creates.

 You can move a file in a single step. Click and drag or tap and drag the file to the desired folder. When the file is over the folder, release the mouse button or lift your finger. Although this method can make moving easier, it can also make it easier to move a file to the wrong destination. Double-check that the file ends up where you want it before going on to other things.

Rename a File or a Folder

1. You can change the name of any file or folder you create. (Don't rename files in the Windows or Program Files folders.) For this exercise, select the Documents library in File Explorer. Then select one of your files.

 To rename more than one file at a time, see the section "Use Check Boxes to Select Files." On completion of the rename operation, the files you selected will share the name you provide; each file will have a unique number added to the name, starting with *(1)*.

2. On the Home tab, select the Rename button. In the content area, the current name of the file or folder is selected, as shown in **Figure 4-17**. If you type anything while the text is selected, you erase the current name, which is convenient if the new name is completely different from the old name. If you want to keep most of the current name and edit it, select inside the name or press the left- or right-arrow key to move to the place in the name where you want to type new text.

Rename your file

Figure 4-17

3. Type the new name, which can be more than 200 characters long (although a dozen characters may be more than enough). You can capitalize letters and use spaces and dashes, but you can't use slashes or asterisks, which Windows 8.1 reserves for other purposes.

> On a touchscreen, the virtual keyboard doesn't appear on the desktop until you select the keyboard icon on the right side of the taskbar.

4. When you've typed the new name, press the Enter key to finish the process.

Delete a File or Folder

1. You can delete any of your files you no longer need. (Don't delete files in the Windows or Program Files folders.) For this exercise, select the Documents folder in File Explorer. Then select one your files.

 To delete more than one file at a time, see the section "Use Check Boxes to Select Files."

2. On the Home tab, select the X on the Delete button.

 The keyboard shortcut to delete the selected file is the Delete key (surprise!).

3. By default, Windows does not provide a confirmation message — your file is gone with a click. A hundred files can be deleted as easily. Select the bottom third of the Delete button to display the drop-down list shown in **Figure 14-18**. Select Show Recycle Confirmation.

Figure 14-18

4. Select another file, and then select the X on the Delete button. The Delete File confirmation window appears. Select Yes to delete the file or No to cancel the operation.

 If the confirmation window seems unnecessary to you, repeat Step 3 to turn off the message.

 You can permanently delete a file, in which case it will not be in the Recycle Bin. Select the file, select the bottom of the Delete button, and then select the Permanently Delete option.

Get Back a File or Folder You Deleted

1. Normally, when you delete a file or folder, Windows 8.1 moves the object to the Recycle Bin. Objects remain in the Recycle Bin indefinitely, allowing you to restore something you deleted long after you did so. In File Explorer, select Desktop under Favorites. To open the Recycle Bin, double-click or double-tap the Recycle Bin in the content area.

 You can open the Recycle Bin also by double-clicking or double-tapping its icon on the desktop itself.

2. If many files or folders are listed in the Recycle Bin window, type the name of the item you want in the Search box in the top-right corner of the window. If any files match what you type, they will appear in the content area.

 On a touchscreen, the virtual keyboard doesn't appear on the desktop until you select the keyboard icon on the right side of the taskbar.

3. To restore a file or folder to its original location, select the file or folder in the Recycle Bin window. On the Manage tab, select Restore the Selected Items, as shown in **Figure 14-19**. The selected file or folder returns to the folder it was in before it was deleted.

 If Windows 8.1 needs disk space, it will automatically clear out the oldest files in the Recycle Bin first. If you want to get rid of everything in the Recycle Bin, select the Manage tab and then select Empty Recycle Bin. After you empty the Recycle Bin, you can't undo your action.

Figure 14-19

 Don't select the Restore All Items button because it puts every single item in the Recycle Bin back in its original location. Most of the files in the Recycle Bin are probably files that you really meant to delete. Choosing this command would be like dumping the trash can on your living-room floor to find a penny you threw away.

 See Chapter 15 for information on backing up and restoring files.

Backing Up and Restoring Files

*S*ome of your files — photos and documents — are priceless. If you accidentally delete a treasured file, what can you do but cry? You can insure your well-being by creating copies of your documents and photos.

The best insurance involves storing copies of files on devices separate from your computer. Such devices include the following:

⟫ **Flash drive and memory card:** Carry your files when you're away from your computer by storing them on a portable storage device. For example, you can store files on a USB *flash drive* (also called a *thumb drive*), which is about the size of a disposable cigarette lighter, or a *memory card*, which is the size of a postage stamp and is most often used in laptop computers and digital cameras. Common capacities for flash drives and memory cards range from 2 to 64GB.

🎯 A *gigabyte* (GB) of storage can hold thousands of files, but you'll be amazed how quickly you can fill that space.

- **External hard drive:** This type of drive has a much higher capacity than a flash drive, making it ideal for backing up all your files — the best insurance. Affordable external hard drives range from 500GB to 3TB.

 A *terabyte* (TB) of storage is equal to a thousand gigabytes, which should be enough room to back up everything on your computer.

- **Network drive:** If your computer connects to a home network, you may be able to copy files to other devices on the network. For example, you could use a large capacity network drive to backup files from more than one computer.

- **SkyDrive:** Your Microsoft account comes with gigabytes of free storage in the cloud (on the Internet). Anything stored in SkyDrive is duplicated on additional computers you log into with the same Microsoft account.

 SkyDrive provides storage but not a backup (duplicate). If you delete a file from SkyDrive, any copies stored on linked computers are also deleted.

In this chapter, you copy files to a flash drive to transport between machines or as an ad hoc backup. You also use the File History function, which automatically copies files as a backup. Consider this scenario: You write a letter to a friend and save it to your Documents folder. Later that day, you delete part of the letter and save it again, replacing the original document. The next day, you wish you still had the deleted text. File History comes to your rescue because it saves versions of files; you can recover the latest version or an earlier version of a file. As I wrote this book, I saved it hundreds of times — File History could save every version, allowing me to rollback to an earlier copy, before I made some big goof. (That's purely hypothetical, of course.)

Finally, you explore the Refresh function, a tool you may need if you have problems with your computer. The Refresh function reinstalls Windows 8.1 but preserves your personal data.

Add an External Hard Drive or Flash Drive

1. Before you attach a flash drive or hard drive to your computer, consider the following options Windows 8.1 automatically offers for using the newly attached disk:

- **Configure This Drive for Backup** uses the new drive for the File History function and is best suited to large-capacity drives, at least 500GB. You would select this option to back up all your files.

- **Open Folder to View Files** displays the contents of the disk in File Explorer on the desktop. You would select this option to copy files to or from the drive you're attaching.

- **Take No Action** dismisses the notification.

 Notifications appear for the amount of time specified in PC Settings. See Chapter 3 for steps to increase the time that notifications appear on screen. If the notification disappears before you can select it, you can redisplay it by removing and then reinserting the drive or USB cable.

2. Locate an unused USB port on your computer. A *USB port* is a small rectangular slot on the front or back of a desktop computer or along any edge of a laptop or tablet computer. USB ports are often marked with a symbol that looks like a trident, as shown in **Figure 15-1**.

USB symbol

USB flash drive   USB port

Figure 15-1

 If a USB port is hard to reach, you can buy an extension cable from any office supply store. You can also buy a *hub*, which adds ports to your computer.

3. If you're using a flash drive, insert it into the USB slot — USB fits one way only. If you're using an external hard drive, plug it into a power source, if one is required, and then connect a cable to the USB port. Turn on the external drive, if it has a separate power switch. (Flash drives and some external hard drives don't have separate power supplies or switches.)

4. Windows 8.1 displays a notification to *Tap to choose what happens with removable drives.* (You can click the mouse instead of tapping.) If you select the first notification, a list of choices appears, as shown in **Figure 15-2**. If you know which action you want to take, you can select that action. Otherwise, select Take No Action or wait until the notification disappears on its own.

Figure 15-2

Copy Files to or from a Flash Drive

1. To copy files or folders to a flash drive, insert the flash drive into one of your computer's USB ports.

 Laptops, like cameras, often have a slot for a memory card. Want to turn your memory card into a flash drive? Simply buy a device called a dedicated or single-purpose memory card reader. Strictly speaking a multipurpose card reader would also work, but multicard readers cost more and are often larger than single-card readers. In addition, a dedicated memory card reader lets you skip using a cable to connect a camera to a computer.

2. If Windows 8.1 displays a notification (refer to **Figure 15-2**) when you insert the flash drive or memory card, select Open Folder to View Files, which will open File Explorer on the desktop. If File Explorer doesn't open automatically, select the Desktop tile on the Start screen, and then select the yellow folder icon in the taskbar.

 The keyboard shortcut to open File Explorer is ⊞+E. You don't need to switch to the desktop before using the shortcut.

3. In File Explorer, navigate on the left to the folder that contains the files you want to copy. See Chapter 14 for information on navigating in File Explorer. Select the folder.

4. On the right side of File Explorer, select the folder or file you want to copy. If you see a check box to the left of each object you want to copy, you can select each check box to copy multiple files at once. (If you don't see check boxes next to files, see Chapter 14 for information on enabling this function for file selection.)

 To select every object on the right at once, use the Select All button on the Home tab. You can also select the files you don't want to copy, and then use the Invert Selection button on the Home tab — deselected files become selected and vice versa. You can select files in other ways as well.

 The keyboard shortcut to select all files in File Explorer is Ctrl+A.

5. In the ribbon, select the Home tab, and then select the Copy To button, as shown in **Figure 15-3**. Select Choose Location from the menu that appears.

Select the Copy To button

Figure 15-3

You can move files if you want them gone from their original location. To do so, select the Move To button. Follow the remaining steps, but substitute the word *Move* for *Copy.*

6. In the Copy Items window, under the Computer heading, locate the flash drive or memory card. The drive will not be Local Disk (C:), where Windows 8.1 resides. Select the flash drive or memory card to which you want to copy the files, as shown in **Figure 15-4,** and then select the Copy button. If the files copy quickly, you may not see any indication of progress; otherwise, a progress bar is displayed until copying is complete.

Select a location for the copy

Figure 15-4

 If you select your user name in the Copy Items dialog box, you may see SkyDrive listed in the expanded list. Files you copy to SkyDrive are automatically copied to the cloud and to linked computers. If you don't see SkyDrive under your user name, see Chapter 12.

7. If you copy a file that is already on the destination disk, the Replace or Skip Files window appears, as shown in **Figure 15-5**. (Perhaps you're copying a newer version of a file you copied before.) Note the available options:

- **Replace the File in the Destination Folder:** Selecting this option replaces one file with another. Be certain you don't need the replaced file (as you might if you want to keep different versions of files).

- **Skip This File:** Selecting this option does nothing with this file.

- **Compare Info for Both Files:** Selecting this option opens another window in which you can select files on the left to replace those on the right and select files on the right to keep. Selecting the same file on the left and right creates a second file with a number added to the name, such as *my file (2)*. This option enables you to have the original and the new file.

Select one of the previous options. If you selected Compare Info for Both Files, select the files to replace or skip, and then select the Continue button. You may or may not see a progress indicator, depending on how quickly the files are copied.

Figure 15-5

8. Confirm that the copy worked by navigating on the left to the location you selected as the destination in Step 6. If the files are there, congratulations; you're done. If not, try Steps 4 through 6 again.

9. Remove the flash drive or memory card you inserted in Step 1. You're good to go.

 If you have files or folders that you'd be devastated to lose, follow the steps in this task to create backup copies of those items on a portable storage device. Then keep that device in a safe place.

 To copy files from a flash drive or memory card, follow these same steps but select the flash drive in Step 3 and the folder or other destination to which you want to copy or move files in Step 6.

Turn On File History

1. To enable Windows 8.1 to create backup copies of the files in your Documents, Music, Pictures, Video, and Desktop folders, type **history** on the Start screen. On the search results panel, select File History Settings and then select File History.

 Another way to access File History is to select Configure This Drive for Backup when you attach an external hard drive. In that event, skip to Step 3.

 File History stores information on an external drive or a network location. After you turn on File History, it will automatically create copies of your documents and photos on the drive you identify. If you lose, delete, or change your mind about changes to a file, you can restore the backup copy created by File History following the steps in the "Restore Files with File History" section, later in this chapter.

2. The File History window opens on the desktop. (See Chapter 5 for information on using the desktop.) File History is off by default. If an external drive is attached, that drive and its free space are listed in the File History window, as shown in **Figure 15-6**. If no drive is displayed, attach one.

Turn on File History

Figure: Update and recovery settings screen

Figure 15-6

> Use the Select a Different Drive function if you want to select a different drive for File History. Use an external drive with at least 40GB of free space — the more free space, the better.

3. If the screen indicates that File History is off, select the Turn On button. Windows 8.1 starts copying files to your hard drive.

4. By default, Windows 8.1 saves copies of files every hour, but you can change this and other file history settings in the Control Panel. Go to the desktop, display the Charm bar, and choose Settings. Then choose Control Panel in the Settings panel. The Control Panel opens. Under System and Security, select Save Backup Copies of Your Files with File History.

5. Select the Advanced Settings function. The screen that appears next (see **Figure** 15-7) provides the following options:

Make your selections here

Figure 15-7

- **Save Copies of Files:** This option controls how frequently File History checks for new or changed files. I recommend that you select Every 10 Minutes to minimize the chances of losing new or changed documents.

- **Size of Offline Cache:** This option applies when you have disconnected the external drive you set up for File History. While that drive is disconnected, an offline cache temporarily stores changes on the internal hard disk. You will probably not need to change this option, especially if you usually leave the external drive attached while you work.

When you go on vacation, consider disconnecting the external drive and storing it in a fireproof safe or a safe deposit box. The drive is your insurance against theft or destruction.

- **Keep Saved Versions:** By default, File History keeps copies of your files forever. This option allows you to limit how long copies are kept. Leave this set as Forever.

- **Clean Up Versions:** This function opens a window in which you select the time period to use to delete older versions of backups. Times range from older than one month to older than two years. (The Keep Saved Versions option uses the same time increments and performs automatically; this function runs only when you choose it.) The All but the Latest One option, which I do not recommend, does not save any previous versions.

6. If you made changes that you want to keep, select the Save Changes button. Otherwise, select Cancel. You return to the main File History window.

Restore Files with File History

1. On the Start screen, type **restore**. On the search results screen, select Restore Your Files with File History. File History opens on the desktop, as shown in **Figure 15-8**.

2. The most recent backup versions created by File History appear in the window. To see other versions of backups, select the left-pointing arrow at the bottom of the window. To return to the most recent backup, select the right-pointing arrow.

Previous (older) backups

Figure 15-8

 Don't select the Restore button until you select the specific file(s) you want. Otherwise, all files will be restored at once.

 Generally, you will want to restore the most recent version of a file. However, if you want to restore content that you changed prior to the most recent version, browse to an earlier backup.

3. If you know the location of the file you want to restore, you can open that location with a double-click or double-tap. If you're not sure of the location, select the search box in the upper-right corner and type the document name. Matching results appear as you type. Select the file you want to restore.

 On a touchscreen, the virtual keyboard doesn't appear on the desktop until you select the keyboard icon on the right side of the taskbar.

4. Select the Restore button. If you restored a file you previously deleted, you can close File History. Skip the remaining steps.

5. If the Replace or Skip Files window opens (refer to **Figure 15-5**) in the preceding step, a version of the file exists in the original location. If you're sure you want to restore the previous version of the file, you could choose Replace the File in the Destination Folder. However, to see additional options, select Compare Info for Both Files. The File Conflict window appears.

6. In the File Conflict window, consider the following selections:

- Select files on the left to replace files in the destination with the backup files. (This is the same as selecting Replace on the Replace or Skip Files screen.)

- Select files on the right to cancel restoring those files. (This is the same as selecting Skip on the Replace or Skip Files screen.)

- If you select the same files on both sides of the window, File History will leave the original as is and restore the backup version with the same name plus *(2)*, allowing you to have both versions. (You need this option only if you're uncertain about which version you want.)

 If you're restoring multiple files at the same time, you can select different options for each: replace one, skip another, and have File History create a copy for another. That's a lot of choices in one little window.

7. Select Continue, and Windows 8.1 completes the operation based on your choices in Step 6. The location of the restored files opens in File Explorer.

Refresh a Misbehaving Computer

1. Glitch happens. The computer misbehaves, a program crashes, or the machine becomes unexpectedly slow. If your computer is misbehaving, try refreshing it. On the Start screen, type **refresh**. Then select Refresh Your PC without Affecting Your Files.

 Before you refresh your PC, see Chapter 12 for information about maintaining Windows 8.1, especially the Action Center and Reliability Monitor. Updating Windows may resolve some problems.

 The Refresh function should leave your data alone and unchanged. However, consider following Steps 1–3 in the section "Restore Files with File History" to confirm that your external drive contains all your files. Better safe than sorry.

 You can also find this function in the General category of PC Settings screen, under the heading Refresh Your PC without Affecting Your Files. Select the Get Started button.

2. On the Refresh Your PC screen, select the Get Started button, as shown in **Figure 15-9**.

 The Refresh function doesn't remove apps installed through the Microsoft Store but does remove any apps you installed any other way. This safety feature is based on the assumption that something you installed from some other source is causing a problem. Be certain that you either don't need a desktop app or you have the materials necessary to reinstall a desktop app, such as Microsoft Office. Windows 8.1 will create a file on the desktop after the fact identifying the programs it removed.

This is where you want to click

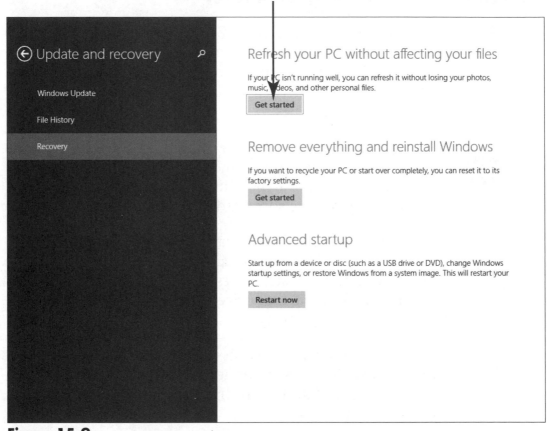

Figure 15-9

3. If you see a message to *Insert media,* Windows 8.1
requires the original installation disc before proceeding.
Insert the Windows 8.1 installation or recover disc in
your CD/DVD drive or plug in a USB drive with this
information. The Refresh function will proceed when you
insert the required media. If you don't have the required
media, select Cancel. (Read the remaining steps.)

4. Select the Refresh button. (Or select Cancel, if you're just
exploring this feature and don't want to continue with it.)

5. Refresh runs and your computer will restart at least once. When the refresh process is complete, the Lock screen appears. Sign in as usual. Select the Desktop tile. If you see a file named *Removed Apps* on the desktop, double-click or double-tap it to open that file in Internet Explorer. The removed apps are listed. If you're aware that one of these apps created a problem, don't reinstall it.

 Don't be intimidated by the Refresh function — it's easy, quick, and worthwhile if it makes a problem computer run better.

Index

• S •

Notes

About the Authors

A computerist for more than 30 years, **Mark Justice Hinton** has written books on digital photography as well as on several versions of Microsoft. This is his fourth title in the *For Seniors* series. He has taught thousands of students since 1988 in classes for the University of New Mexico Division of Continuing Education. Mark writes a blog on computer topics at www.mjhinton.com/help.

Peter Weverka is the best-selling author of many *For Dummies* books, including *Office 2013 All-in-One For Dummies*, as well as 41 other computer books about various topics. Peter's humorous articles and stories (none related to computers, thankfully) have appeared in *Harper's, SPY*, and other magazines for grown-ups.

Dedication

To New Mexico/The Land of Enchantment

Authors' Acknowledgments

It took a lot of people to put this book into your hands. The authors get the fame, the fans, and the fat check, but they couldn't do it without many other people, too many of whom go unnamed here. Thanks to everyone at Wiley for their part in producing this book. Special thanks to Peter Weverka, who updated the book, and Tonya Maddox Cupp, who copy edited it. I also want to thank technical editor Russ Mullen. My deepest thanks, always, to Merri Rudd, photographer and writer.

Publisher's Acknowledgments

Executive Editor: Steven Hayes

Project Editor: Tonya Maddox Cupp

Technical Editor: Russ Mullen

Editorial Assistant: Anne Sullivan

Sr. Editorial Assistant: Cherie Case

Project Coordinator: Sheree Montgomery

Cover Image: ©Image Source/Dan Pangbourne

ple & Mac

ad For Dummies,
h Edition
78-1-118-49823-1

hone 5 For Dummies,
h Edition
78-1-118-35201-4

acBook For Dummies,
h Edition
78-1-118-20920-2

S X Mountain Lion
r Dummies
78-1-118-39418-2

ogging & Social Media

cebook For Dummies,
h Edition
78-1-118-09562-1

om Blogging
r Dummies
78-1-118-03843-7

nterest For Dummies
8-1-118-32800-2

ordPress For Dummies,
n Edition
8-1-118-38318-6

siness

mmodities For Dummies,
d Edition
8-1-118-01687-9

vesting For Dummies,
n Edition
8-0-470-90545-6

Personal Finance
For Dummies,
7th Edition
978-1-118-11785-9

QuickBooks 2013
For Dummies
978-1-118-35641-8

Small Business Marketing Kit
For Dummies,
3rd Edition
978-1-118-31183-7

Careers

Job Interviews
For Dummies,
4th Edition
978-1-118-11290-8

Job Searching with
Social Media
For Dummies
978-0-470-93072-4

Personal Branding
For Dummies
978-1-118-11792-7

Resumes For Dummies,
6th Edition
978-0-470-87361-8

Success as a Mediator
For Dummies
978-1-118-07862-4

Diet & Nutrition

Belly Fat Diet For Dummies
978-1-118-34585-6

Eating Clean For Dummies
978-1-118-00013-7

Nutrition For Dummies,
5th Edition
978-0-470-93231-5

Digital Photography

Digital Photography
For Dummies,
7th Edition
978-1-118-09203-3

Digital SLR Cameras &
Photography For Dummies,
4th Edition
978-1-118-14489-3

Photoshop Elements 11
For Dummies
978-1-118-40821-6

Gardening

Herb Gardening
For Dummies,
2nd Edition
978-0-470-61778-6

Vegetable Gardening
For Dummies,
2nd Edition
978-0-470-49870-5

Health

Anti-Inflammation Diet
For Dummies
978-1-118-02381-5

Diabetes For Dummies,
3rd Edition
978-0-470-27086-8

Living Paleo For Dummies
978-1-118-29405-5

Hobbies

Beekeeping
For Dummies
978-0-470-43065-1

eBay For Dummies,
7th Edition
978-1-118-09806-6

Raising Chickens
For Dummies
978-0-470-46544-8

Wine For Dummies,
5th Edition
978-1-118-28872-6

Writing Young Adult Fiction
For Dummies
978-0-470-94954-2

Language & Foreign Language

500 Spanish Verbs
For Dummies
978-1-118-02382-2

English Grammar
For Dummies,
2nd Edition
978-0-470-54664-2

French All-in One
For Dummies
978-1-118-22815-9

German Essentials
For Dummies
978-1-118-18422-6

Italian For Dummies
2nd Edition
978-1-118-00465-4

e Available in print and e-book formats.

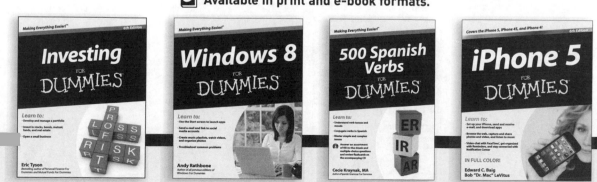

ilable wherever books are sold. For more information or to order direct: U.S. customers visit www.Dummies.com or call 1-877-762-2974.
U.K. customers visit www.Wileyeurope.com or call (0) 1243 843291. Canadian customers visit www.Wiley.ca or call 1-800-567-4797.

Connect with us online at www.facebook.com/fordummies or @fordummies

Math & Science

Algebra I For Dummies,
2nd Edition
978-0-470-55964-2

Anatomy and Physiology
For Dummies,
2nd Edition
978-0-470-92326-9

Astronomy For Dummies,
3rd Edition
978-1-118-37697-3

Biology For Dummies,
2nd Edition
978-0-470-59875-7

Chemistry For Dummies,
2nd Edition
978-1-1180-0730-3

Pre-Algebra Essentials
For Dummies
978-0-470-61838-7

Microsoft Office

Excel 2013 For Dummies
978-1-118-51012-4

Office 2013 All-in-One
For Dummies
978-1-118-51636-2

PowerPoint 2013
For Dummies
978-1-118-50253-2

Word 2013 For Dummies
978-1-118-49123-2

Music

Blues Harmonica
For Dummies
978-1-118-25269-7

Guitar For Dummies,
3rd Edition
978-1-118-11554-1

iPod & iTunes
For Dummies,
10th Edition
978-1-118-50864-0

Programming

Android Application
Development For
Dummies, 2nd Edition
978-1-118-38710-8

iOS 6 Application
Development For Dummies
978-1-118-50880-0

Java For Dummies,
5th Edition
978-0-470-37173-2

Religion & Inspiration

The Bible For Dummies
978-0-7645-5296-0

Buddhism For Dummies,
2nd Edition
978-1-118-02379-2

Catholicism For Dummies,
2nd Edition
978-1-118-07778-8

Self-Help & Relationships

Bipolar Disorder
For Dummies,
2nd Edition
978-1-118-33882-7

Meditation For Dummies,
3rd Edition
978-1-118-29144-3

Seniors

Computers For Seniors
For Dummies,
3rd Edition
978-1-118-11553-4

iPad For Seniors
For Dummies,
5th Edition
978-1-118-49708-1

Social Security
For Dummies
978-1-118-20573-0

Smartphones & Tablets

Android Phones
For Dummies
978-1-118-16952-0

Kindle Fire HD
For Dummies
978-1-118-42223-6

NOOK HD For Dummies,
Portable Edition
978-1-118-39498-4

Surface For Dummies
978-1-118-49634-3

Test Prep

ACT For Dummies,
5th Edition
978-1-118-01259-8

ASVAB For Dummies,
3rd Edition
978-0-470-63760-9

GRE For Dummies,
7th Edition
978-0-470-88921-3

Officer Candidate Tests,
For Dummies
978-0-470-59876-4

Physician's Assistant Exa
For Dummies
978-1-118-11556-5

Series 7 Exam
For Dummies
978-0-470-09932-2

Windows 8

Windows 8 For Dummies
978-1-118-13461-0

Windows 8 For Dummies
Book + DVD Bundle
978-1-118-27167-4

Windows 8 All-in-One
For Dummies
978-1-118-11920-4

Available in print and e-book formats.

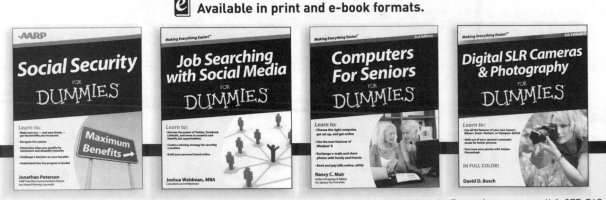

Take Dummies with you everywhere you go!

Whether you're excited about e-books, want more from the web, must have your mobile apps, or swept up in social media, Dummies makes everything easier .

Dummies products make life easier

- DIY ~~WITHDRAWN~~
- Consumer Electronics
- Crafts
- Software
- Cookware
- Hobbies
- Videos
- Music
- Games
- and More!

For more information, go to **Dummies.com®** and search the store by category.

FOR
DUMMIES
A Wiley Bra